ROUTLEDGE LIBRARY EDITIONS: 18TH CENTURY LITERATURE

Volume 3

THE WOMAN'S VIEW

THE WOMAN'S VIEW

An Anthology of
Prose Passages about Women,
from the Eighteenth Century
to the Present Day

Edited by
JUNE WEDGWOOD BENN

LONDON AND NEW YORK

First published in 1967 by Routledge & Kegan Paul Ltd

This edition first published in 2020
by Routledge
2 Park Square, Milton Park, Abingdon, Oxon OX14 4RN

and by Routledge
52 Vanderbilt Avenue, New York, NY 10017

Routledge is an imprint of the Taylor & Francis Group, an informa business

© 1967 June Wedgwood Benn

All rights reserved. No part of this book may be reprinted or reproduced or utilised in any form or by any electronic, mechanical, or other means, now known or hereafter invented, including photocopying and recording, or in any information storage or retrieval system, without permission in writing from the publishers.

Trademark notice: Product or corporate names may be trademarks or registered trademarks, and are used only for identification and explanation without intent to infringe.

British Library Cataloguing in Publication Data
A catalogue record for this book is available from the British Library

ISBN: 978-0-367-44270-5 (Set)
ISBN: 978-1-00-302027-1 (Set) (ebk)
ISBN: 978-0-367-86032-5 (Volume 3) (hbk)
ISBN: 978-0-367-86035-6 (Volume 3) (pbk)
ISBN: 978-1-00-301654-0 (Volume 3) (ebk)

Publisher's Note
The publisher has gone to great lengths to ensure the quality of this reprint but points out that some imperfections in the original copies may be apparent.

Disclaimer
The publisher has made every effort to trace copyright holders and would welcome correspondence from those they have been unable to trace.

The Woman's View

An anthology of prose passages about women, from the eighteenth century to the present day

edited by
JUNE WEDGWOOD BENN

London: Routledge & Kegan Paul

*First published 1967
by Routledge & Kegan Paul Ltd
Broadway House, 68-74 Carter Lane
London, E.C.4.*

*Printed and Bound in Great Britain by
Willmer Brothers Limited, Birkenhead*

© *June Wedgwood Benn 1967*

*No part of this book may be reproduced
in any form without permission from
the publisher, except for the quotation
of brief passages in criticism*

SBN 7100 6005 X

CONTENTS

		page
	Acknowledgments	vi
	Introduction	vii
1	YOUNG GIRLS from *The House in Paris* by Elizabeth Bowen	1
2	DIFFERENT GIRLS from *The Waves* by Virginia Woolf	2
3	BEING A GIRL from *Memoirs of a Dutiful Daughter* by Simone de Beauvoir	6
4	GROWING UP I from *The Member of the Wedding* by Carson McCullers	8
5	GROWING UP II from *The Rainbow* by D. H. Lawrence	14
6	WANTING A CHANCE IN LIFE from *The Story of an African Farm* by Olive Schreiner	17
7	WANTING SOMETHING MORE from *Jane Eyre* by Charlotte Brontë	19
8	A YOUNG GIRL'S ASPIRATIONS from *Journals* by Marie Bashkirtseff	21
9	BEING NON-EDUCATED from *Letters* by Mary Kingsley	24
10	WEAK WOMAN from *A Vindication of the Rights of Women* by Mary Wollstonecraft	28
11	BEING IN LOVE I from *Emma* by Jane Austen	30
12	PLANNING FOR THE FUTURE from *Middlemarch* by George Eliot	32

13	BEING A GOVERNESS from *Agnes Grey* by Anne Brontë	35
14	BEING ENGAGED from *The Egoist* by George Meredith	44
15	MARRIAGE FOR THE WRONG REASONS— OR TO THE WRONG MAN from *Portrait of a Lady* by Henry James	49
16	LOVE AND COMMONSENSE from *Letters* by Jane Austen	52
17	ADVISING A DAUGHTER ON LIFE from *Letters* by Queen Victoria	56
18	BEING MARRIED from *At the Bay* by Katherine Mansfield	60
19	BEING MARRIED—AND A LITTLE OLDER from *To The Lighthouse* by Virginia Woolf	64
20	BEING A BLUESTOCKING MARRIED TO A GENIUS from *Letters* by Jane Welsh Carlyle	68
21	WANTING A LIFE OF ONE'S OWN from *All Passion Spent* by Victoria Sackville-West	71
22	ESCAPING TEMPORARILY from *A View of the Harbour* by Elizabeth Taylor	76
23	HOW LIFE PASSES from *Tenterhooks* by Ada Leverson	80
24	COMING UP FOR AIR from *Dangerous Ages* by Rose Macaulay	87
25	BIRD IN A CAGE from *A Doll's House* by Henrik Ibsen	89
26	BEING AN OUTSIDER from *The Holiday* by Stevie Smith	93
27	BEING DISSATISFIED WITH THE LOVE OF MAN from *The Echoing Grove* by Rosamond Lehmann	95
28	BEING A SENSITIVE SOUL from *Howards End* by E. M. Forster	97

29	LOVING from *The Woodlanders* by Thomas Hardy	99
30	BEING IN LOVE II from *Letters to Imlay* by Mary Wollstonecraft	101
31	MAN'S IDEAL WIFE — AND LATER from *Middlemarch* by George Eliot	104
32	MAN'S IDEAL OF WOMAN from *An Ideal Husband* by Oscar Wilde	108
33	WOMAN PLAYING UP TO HER ROLE from *An Ideal Husband* by Oscar Wilde	110
34	THE SHAVIAN IDEAL OF WOMAN AND MAN from *Man and Superman* by George Bernard Shaw	112
35	BEING A 'FREE' WOMAN from *My Life* by Isadora Duncan	116
36	BRINGING UP A BABY from *A Proper Marriage* by Doris Lessing	118
37	A MAN INFATUATED — AND OUT OF LOVE from *Liber Amoris* by William Hazlitt	125
38	BEING A MOTHER from *Look the Other Way* by John Branfield	129
39	A MAN IN TWO MINDS from *Nightmare Abbey* by Thomas Love Peacock	143
40	IF SHAKESPEARE HAD BEEN A WOMAN from *A Room of One's Own* by Virginia Woolf	146
41	BEING A POLITICAL WOMAN from *The New Machiavelli* by H. G. Wells	150
42	WOMEN AND FICTION from *Granite and Rainbow* by Virginia Woolf	156
43	WOMAN IN PRESENT SOCIETY from *'The Guardian'* by Mary Stott	160
	Suggestions for Oral Discussion or Written Work	163
	Suggestions for Further Reading	167

ACKNOWLEDGMENTS

Acknowledgments are made to the following for permission to reproduce copyright material: The Society of Authors and Miss Rosamond Lehmann for an extract from *The Echoing Grove;* A. D. Peters and Co., for an extract from *Dangerous Ages* by Rose Macaulay; Chapman & Hall Ltd., for the passage from *The Holiday* by Stevie Smith; John Branfield and Eyre and Spottiswoode Ltd., for a chapter from *Look the Other Way;* Liveright Publishing Corp., New York for extracts from *My Life* by Isadora Duncan; Macmillan & Co., for the passages from the diary of Mary Kingsley from *The Life of Mary Kingsley* by Stephen Gwynn; The Public Trustee and the Society of Authors for the extracts from *Man and Superman* by G. B. Shaw; to Ernest Benn Ltd., for the extract from Olive Schreiner's *The Story of an African Farm;* the executors of H. G. Wells for an extract from *The New Machiavelli;* the Trustees of the Hardy Estate and Macmillan & Co. Ltd., for an extract from *The Woodlanders* by Thomas Hardy; Laurence Pollinger Ltd., and the Estate of the late Mrs. Frieda Lawrence for an extract from *The Rainbow* by D. H. Lawrence; Carson McCullers and the Cresset Press for an extract from *The Member of the Wedding;* Doris Lessing and MacGibbon & Kee Ltd., for an extract from *A Proper Marriage* by Doris Lessing; MacGibbon & Kee Ltd., for an extract from *The Little Ottleys* by Ada Leverson; E. M. Forster and Edward Arnold Ltd., for the passage from *Howard's End;* Elizabeth Bowen and Jonathan Cape Ltd., for an extract from *The House in Paris* by Elizabeth Bowen; Elizabeth Taylor for an extract from *A View of the Harbour;* Leonard Woolf and The Hogarth Press Ltd., for the four extracts from the works of Virginia Woolf; the Literary Executors of the late Sackville West and The Hogarth Press Ltd., for the extract from *All Passions Spent; The Guardian* for an extract from the *Guardian's* Woman's Page; Roger Fulford and Evans Bros. Ltd., for extracts from *Dearest Child;* Lady Bliss for an extract from her book *The Letters of Jane Welsh Carlyle;* Andre Deutsch Ltd., for the extract from S. de Beauvoir's *Memoirs of a Dutiful Daughter,* and to the Society of Authors as the Literary Representative of the Estate of the late Katherine Mansfield for the extracts from *At the Bay.*

INTRODUCTION

This anthology is intended for girls who are taking English, either for General Studies or in preparation for university. The extracts cover a wide range of styles and periods. We hope that each one is lively and interesting enough in itself and sufficiently representative of its author's work and standpoint to encourage further reading.

The linked theme is that of being a woman—in society, in the home and as a person in one's own right. The passages are only an infinitesimal sample of nineteenth and twentieth century literature on the subject. For those who are deeply interested, the works of Virginia Woolf in English, Simone de Beauvoir in French and George Eliot for a view back to the nineteenth century are indispensable.

In these days of emancipation and assumed equality (in some countries at any rate) it is as well to remember the very recent past and to look forward to the future, for *all* girls will have certain problems to face just because they are girls. It is best to be prepared.

The questions and points for discussion are only *suggestions* for essay work or oral discussion and points of departure for argument. All the passages may be used for textual analysis or linguistic commentary according to the teacher's whim and depending on the different intellectual levels of the students. Should there be male students in the class it is to be hoped they will not be too bored or too complacent but will begin to understand the 'woman's view'.

A word to students

If any of these extracts take your fancy ask your teacher where to find the whole work or to suggest other books by the same writer. The women's pages of *The Guardian* and *The Times* are well worth studying. The biographies are not exhaustive. Try to think of other ideas for discussion suggested by the passages. Half of the extracts are from twentieth-century writers, though you may not have heard of all of them. Many of the books are not at all heavy going, and will entertain you, as well as teach you something.

The compiler's aim has been to bring 'life' and 'literature' together since at school they so often appear to be poles apart. So please do not regard the book in the way you do a 'set-text', but try to visualise the human being behind the writer and to conceive of problems and situations which you may be lucky not to have—or yet have!—yourself.

1 Young Girls

From *The House in Paris*

by Elizabeth Bowen

Elizabeth Bowen was born in Dublin and her first book, Encounters *was published in 1923. She has written many novels and short stories. Some of the best are* The Last September, *1929,* Friends and Relations, *1931,* To The North, *1932 and* The House in Paris, *1935. (See also other titles for recommended reading at the back of this book.)*

She is what critics term a 'feminine' writer, whatever this means. She is certainly a pronounced stylist. In her short stories a supernatural element is present but her best novels are delicate studies of shifting human relationships. She writes especially well about young girls.

The House in Paris *unveils the past through the present eyes of two small children staying for different reasons for a day at a relative's house.*

She thought, young girls like the excess of any quality. Without knowing, they want to suffer, to suffer they must exaggerate; they like to have loud chords struck on them. Loving art better than life they need men to be actors; only an actor moves them, with his telling smile, undomestic, out of touch with the everyday that they dread. They love to enjoy love as a system of doubts and shocks. They are right: not seeking husbands yet, they have no reason to see love socially. This natural fleshly protest against good taste is broken down soon enough; their natural love of the cad is outwitted by their mothers. Vulgarity, inborn like original sin, unfolds with the woman nature, unfolds ahead of it quickly and has a flamboyant flowering in the young girl. Wise mothers do not nip it immediately; that makes for trouble later, they watch it out.

2 Different Girls

From *The Waves*

by Virginia Woolf

Virginia Woolf (1882–1941) was a granddaughter of the novelist Thackeray and wrote many novels and much literary criticism. With her husband Leonard Woolf she founded the Hogarth Press. She was very much concerned with the lives of women and their position in society though her novels are far removed from tub-thumping. Some think her best novel was the most experimental, The Waves, *(1931). She suffered from attacks of mental depression all her life and committed suicide in 1941.*

The Waves *is the story of a contrasted group of friends.*

A Room of One's Own *is a plea for solitude and a private income for the woman writer.*

To The Lighthouse *introduces Mrs. Ramsay, a woman who lives for her family and yet has aspirations of her own.*

Granite and Rainbow *is a posthumous collection of essays.*

'I have torn off the whole of May and June,' said Susan, 'and twenty days of July. I have torn them off and screwed them up so that they no longer exist, save as a weight in my side. They have been crippled days, like moths with shrivelled wings unable to fly. There are only eight days left. In eight days' time I shall get out of the train and stand on the platform at six twenty-five. Then my freedom will unfurl, and all these restrictions that wrinkle and shrivel—hours and order and discipline, and being here and there exactly at the right moment—will crack asunder. Out the day will spring as I open the carriage-door and see my father in his old hat and gaiters. I shall tremble. I shall burst into tears. Then next morning I shall get up at dawn. I shall let myself out by the kitchen door. I shall walk on the moor. The great horses of the phantom riders will thunder behind me and stop suddenly. I shall see the swallow skim the grass. I shall throw myself on a bank by the river and watch the fish slip in and out among the reeds. The palms of my hands will be printed with pine-needles. I shall there unfold and take out whatever it is I have made here; something hard. For something has grown in me here, through the winters and summers, on staircases, in bedrooms. I do not want, as Jinny wants, to be admired. I do not want people, when I come in, to look up with admiration. I want to give, to be given, and solitude in which to unfold my possessions.

'Then I shall come back through the trembling lanes under the arches of the nut leaves. I shall pass an old woman wheeling a perambulator full of sticks; and the shepherd. But we shall not speak. I shall come back through the kitchen garden, and see the curved leaves of the cabbages pebbled with dew, and the house in the garden, blind with curtained windows. I shall go upstairs to my room, and turn over my own things, locked carefully in the wardrobe: my shells; my eggs; my curious grasses. I shall feed my doves and my squirrel. I shall go to the kennel and comb my spaniel. So gradually I shall turn over the hard thing that has grown here in my side. But here bells ring; feet shuffle perpetually.'

'I hate darkness and sleep and night,' said Jinny, 'and lie longing for the day to come. I long that the week should be all one day without divisions. When I wake early—and the birds wake me—I lie and watch the brass handles on the cupboard grow clear; then the basin; then the towel-horse. As each thing in the bedroom grows clear, my heart beats quicker. I feel my body harden, and become pink, yellow, brown. My hands pass over my legs and body. I feel its slope, its thinness. I love to hear the gong roar through the house and the stir begin—here a thud, there a patter. Doors slam; water rushes. Here is another day, here is another day, I cry, as my feet touch the floor. It may be a bruised day, an imperfect day. I am often scolded. I am often in disgrace for idleness, for laughing; but even as Miss Matthews grumbles at my feather-headed carelessness, I catch sight of something moving—a speck of sun perhaps on a picture, or the donkey drawing the mowing-machine across the lawn; or a sail that passes between the laurel leaves, so that I am never cast down. I cannot be prevented from pirouetting behind Miss Matthews into prayers.

'Now, too, the time is coming when we shall leave school and wear long skirts. I shall wear necklaces and a white dress without sleeves at night. There will be parties in brilliant rooms; and one man will single me out and will tell me what he has told no other person. He will like me better than Susan or Rhoda. He will find in me some quality, some peculiar thing. But I shall not let myself be attached to one person only. I do not want to be fixed, to be pinioned. I tremble, I quiver, like the leaf in the hedge, as I sit dangling my feet, on the edge of the bed, with a new day to break open. I have fifty years, I have sixty years to spend. I have not broken into my hoard. This is the beginning.'

'There are hours and hours,' said Rhoda, 'before I can put out the light and lie suspended on my bed above the world, before I can let the day drop down, before I can let my tree grow, quivering in green pavilions above my head. Here I cannot let it grow. Somebody knocks through it. They ask questions, they interrupt, they throw it down.

'Now I will go to the bathroom and take off my shoes and wash; but as I wash, as I bend my head down over the basin, I will let the Russian Empress's veil flow about my shoulders. The diamonds of the Imperial crown blaze on my forehead. I hear the roar of the hostile mob as I step out on to the balcony. Now I dry my hands, vigorously, so that Miss, whose name I forget, cannot suspect that I am waving my fist at an infuriated mob. "I am your Empress, people." My attitude is one of defiance, I am fearless. I conquer.

'But this is a thin dream. This is a papery tree. Miss Lambert blows it down. Even the sight of her vanishing down the corridor blows it to atoms. It is not solid; it gives me no satisfaction—this Empress dream. It leaves me, now that it has fallen, here in the passage rather shivering.

Things seem paler. I will go now into the library and take out some book, and read and look; and read again and look. Here is a poem about a hedge. I will wander down it and pick flowers, green cowbind and the moonlight-coloured May, wild roses and ivy serpentine. I will clasp them in my hands and lay them on the desk's shiny surface. I will sit by the river's trembling edge and look at the water-lilies, broad and bright, which lit the oak that overhung the hedge with moonlight beams of their own watery light. I will pick flowers; I will bind flowers in one garland and clasp them and present them—Oh! to whom? There is some check in the flow of my being; a deep stream presses on some obstacle; it jerks; it tugs; some knot in the centre resists. Oh, this is pain, this is anguish! I faint, I fail. Now my body thaws; I am unsealed, I am incandescent. Now the stream pours in a deep tide fertilizing, opening the shut, forcing the tight-folded, flooding free. To whom shall I give all that now flows through me, from my warm, my porous body? I will gather my flowers and present them—Oh! to whom?

'Sailors loiter on the parade, and amorous couples; the omnibuses rattle along the sea front to the town. I will give; I will enrich; I will return to the world this beauty. I will bind my flowers in one garland and advancing with my hand outstretched will present them—Oh! to whom?'

3 Being a Girl

From *Memoirs of a Dutiful Daughter*

by Simone de Beauvoir

Simone de Beauvoir was born in 1908 and is a novelist, philosopher and essayist. Le Deuxième Sexe, *1949, a study of women and* Les Mandarins, *(a novel), 1954, are some of her best work. Her autobiography has been translated into English (three volumes so far). This extract is taken from the first volume.* (Memoirs of a Dutiful Daughter, The Prime of Life, Force of Circumstances).

She is an atheist, a socialist and a feminist and since her twenties the companion of Jean-Paul Sartre, the philosopher and exponent of existentialism in France. Simone de Beauvoir has also written many works of criticism and travel-diaries.

I certainly didn't regret being a woman; on the contrary it afforded me great satisfaction. My upbringing had convinced me of my sex's intellectual inferiority, a fact admitted by many women. 'A lady cannot hope to pass the selective examination until the fifth or sixth attempt,' Mademoiselle Rollin had told me; she had already had two. This handicap gave my successes a prestige far in excess of that accorded to successful male students: I felt it was something exceptional even to do as well as they did; in fact, I hadn't met a single man student who seemed at all out of the ordinary; the future was as wide open to me as it was to them: they had no advantage over me. Nor did they lay claim to any; they treated me without condescension, and even with a special kindness, for they didn't look upon me as a rival; girls were judged in the contest by the same standard as the boys, but they were accepted as supernumeraries, and there was no struggle for the first places between the sexes. That is why a lecture I gave on Plato brought me unreserved compliments from my fellow-students—in particular from Jean Hippolyte. I was proud at having won their esteem. Their friendliness prevented me from ever taking up that 'challenging' attitude which later was to cause me so much dismay when I encountered it in American women: from the start, men were my comrades, not my enemies. Far from envying them, I felt that my own position, from the very fact that it was an unusual one, was one of privilege. One evening Pradelle invited to his house his best friends and their sisters. Poupette* went with me. All the girls retired to Mademoiselle Pradelle's room; but I stayed with the young men.

Yet I did not renounce my femininity. That evening my sister and I had paid the utmost attention to our appearance. I was in red, she in blue silk; actually we were very badly got-up, but then the other girls weren't all that grand either. In Montparnasse I had caught glimpses of elegant beauties; but their lives were too different from mine for the comparison to overwhelm me; besides once I was free, with money in my pocket, there would be nothing to stop me imitating them. I didn't forget that Jacques had said I was pretty: Stephen and Fernando had high hopes of me. I liked to look at myself, just as I was, in mirrors; I liked what I saw. In the things we had in common, I fancied that I was no less ill-equipped than other women and I felt no resentment towards them; so I had no desire to run them down. In many respects I set Zaza, my sister, Stephen and even Lisa above my masculine friends, for they seemed to me more sensitive, more generous, more endowed with imagination, tears and love. I flattered myself that I combined 'a woman's heart and a man's brain'. Again I considered myself to be unique—the One and Only.

* S. de Beauvoir's sister.

4 Growing Up I

From *The Member of the Wedding*

by Carson McCullers

Carson McCullers was born in Columbus, Georgia, U.S.A., in 1917. Her books include: The Heart is a Lonely Hunter, 1940, Reflections in a Golden Eye, 1941, The Member of the Wedding, 1946, The Ballad of the Sad Café, 1951, Clock without Hands, 1961.

The Member of the Wedding *(which has been made into a film) is about the first painful beginnings of growing-up in its heroine, Frankie.*

This was the summer when Frankie was sick and tired of being Frankie. She hated herself and had become a loafer and a big no-good who hung around the summer kitchen: dirty and greedy and mean and sad. Besides being too mean to live, she was a criminal. If the Law knew about her, she could be tried in the courthouse and locked up in the jail. Yet Frankie had not always been a criminal and a big no-good. Until the April of that year, and all the years of her life before, she had been like other people. She belonged to a club and was in the seventh grade at school. She worked for her father on Saturday morning and went to the show every Saturday afternoon. She was not the kind of person ever to think of being afraid. At night she slept in the bed with her father, but not because she was scared of the dark.

Then the spring of that year had been a long queer season. Things began to change and Frankie did not understand the change. After the plain grey winter the March winds banged on the window panes, and clouds were shined and white on the blue sky. April that year came sudden and still, and the green of the trees was a wild bright green. The pale wistarias bloomed all over town, and silently the blossoms shattered. There was something about the green trees and the flowers of April that made Frankie sad. She did not know why she was sad, but because of this peculiar sadness, she began to realise she ought to leave the town. She read the war news and thought about the world and packed her suitcase to go away; but she did not know where she should go.

It was the year when Frankie thought about the world. And she did not see it as a round school globe, with the countries neat and different—coloured. She thought of the world as huge and cracked and loose and turning a thousand miles an hour. The geography book at school was out-of-date; the countries of the world had changed. Frankie read the war news in the paper, but there were so many foreign places, and the war was happening so fast, that sometimes she did not understand. It was the summer when Patton was chasing the Germans across France. And they were fighting, too, in Russia and Saipan. She saw the battles, and the soldiers. But there were too many different battles, and she could not see in her mind the millions and millions of soldiers all at once. She saw one Russian soldier, dark and frozen with a frozen gun, in Russian snow. The single Japs with slanted eyes on a jungle island gliding among green vines. Europe and the people hung in trees and the battleships on the blue oceans. Four-motor planes and burning cities and a soldier in a steel war-helmet, laughing. Sometimes these pictures of the war, the world, whirled in her mind and she was dizzy. A long time ago she had predicted that it would take two months to win the whole war, but now she did not know. She wanted to be a boy and go to the war as a Marine. She thought about flying aeroplanes and winning gold medals for bravery. But she could not join the war, and this made her sometimes feel restless and blue. She decided to donate blood to the Red Cross; she wanted to donate a quart a week and her blood would be in the veins of Australians and Fighting French and Chinese, all over the whole world, and it would be as though she were close kin to all these people. She could hear the army doctors saying that the blood of Frankie

Addams was the reddest and strongest blood that they had ever known. And she could picture ahead, in the years after the war, meeting the soldiers who had her blood, and they would say that they owed their life to her; and they would not call her Frankie—they would call her Addams. But this plan for donating her blood to the war did not come true. The Red Cross would not take her blood. She was too young. Frankie felt mad with the Red Cross, and left out of everything.

The war and the world were too fast and big and strange. To think about the world for very long made her afraid. She was not afraid of Germans or bombs or Japanese. She was afraid because in the war they would not include her, and because the world seemed somehow separate from herself.

So she knew she ought to leave the town and go to some place far away. For the late spring, that year, was lazy and too sweet. The long afternoons flowered and lasted and the green sweetness sickened her. The town began to hurt Frankie. Sad and terrible happenings had never made Frankie cry, but this season many things made Frankie suddenly wish to cry. Very early in the morning, she would sometimes go out into the yard and stand for a long time looking at the sunrise sky. And it was as though a question came into her heart, and the sky did not answer. Things she had never noticed much before began to hurt her; home lights watched from the evening sidewalks, an unknown voice from an alley. She would stare at the lights and listen to the voice, and something inside her stiffened and waited. But the lights would darken, the voice fall silent, and though she waited, that was all. She was afraid of these things that made her suddenly wonder who she was, and what she was going to be in the world, and why she was standing at that minute, seeing a light, or listening, or staring up into the sky: alone. She was afraid, and there was a queer tightness in her chest.

One night in April, when she and her father were going to bed, he looked at her and said, all of a sudden: 'Who is this great big long-legged twelve year old blunderbuss who still wants to sleep with her old Papa.' And she was too big to sleep with her father any more. She had to sleep in her upstairs room alone. She began to have a grudge against her father and they looked at each other in a slant-eyed way. She did not like to stay at home.

She went around town, and the things she saw and heard seemed to be left somehow unfinished, and there was the tightness in her that would not break. She would hurry to do something, but what she did was always wrong. She would call her best friend, Evelyn Owen, who owned a football suit and a Spanish shawl, and one would dress in the football suit and the other in the Spanish shawl and they would go down to the ten-cent store together. But that was a wrong thing and not what Frankie wanted. Or after the pale spring twilights, with the smell of dust and flowers sweet and bitter in the air, evenings of lighted windows and the long drawn calls at supper-time, when the chimney swifts had gathered and whirled above the town and flown off somewhere to their home together, leaving the sky empty and wide; after the long twilights of this season, when Frankie had walked around the side-walks of the town, a jazz sadness quirked her nerves and her heart stiffened and almost stopped.

Because she could not break this tightness gathering within her, she would hurry to do something. She would go home and put the coal-scuttle on her head, like a crazy person's hat, and walk around the kitchen table. She would do anything that suddenly occurred to her—but whatever she did was always wrong, and not at all what she had wanted. Then, having done these wrong and silly things, she would stand, sickened and empty, in the kitchen door and say:

'I just wish I could tear down this whole town.'

'Well, tear it down, then. But quit hanging around here with that gloomy face. Do something.'

And finally the troubles started.

She did things and she got herself into trouble. She broke the law. And having once become a criminal, she broke the law again, and then again. She took the pistol from her father's bureau drawer and carried it all over town and shot up the cartridges in a vacant lot. She changed into a robber and stole a three-way knife from the Sears and Roebuck Store. One Saturday afternoon in May she committed a secret and unknown sin. In the MacKean's garage, with Barney MacKean, they committed a queer sin and how bad it was she did not know. The sin made a shrivelling sickness in her stomach, and she dreaded the eyes of everyone. She hated Barney and wanted to kill him. Sometimes alone in the bed at night she planned to shoot him with the pistol or throw a knife between his eyes.

Her best friend, Evelyn Owen, moved away to Florida, and Frankie did not play with anybody any more. The long and flowering spring was over and the summer in the town was ugly and lonesome and very hot. Every day she wanted more and more to leave the town: to light out for South America or Hollywood or New York City. But although she packed her suitcase many times, she could never decide to which of these places she ought to go, or how she would get there by herself.

So she stayed home and hung around the kitchen, and the summer did not end. By dog-days she was five-feet five and three-quarter inches tall, a great big greedy loafer who was too mean to live. She was afraid, but not as she had been before. There was only the fear of Barney, her father, and the Law. But even these fears were finally gone; after a long time the sin in the MacKean's garage became far from her and was remembered only in her dreams. And she would not think of her father or the Law. She stuck close in the kitchen with John Henry and Berenice. She did not think about the war, the world. Nothing hurt her any longer, she did not care. She never stood alone in the backyard in order to stare up at the sky. She paid no attention to sounds and summer voices, and did not walk the streets of town at night. She would not let things make her sad and she would not care. She ate and wrote shows and practised throwing knives against the side of the garage and played bridge at the kitchen table. Every day was like the day before, except that it was longer, and nothing hurt her any more.

So that Friday when it happened, when her brother and the bride came to the house, Frankie knew that everything was changed; but why this was so, and what would happen to her next, she did not know.

5 Growing Up II

From *The Rainbow*

by D. H. Lawrence

D. H. Lawrence (1885–1930) was born in Nottinghamshire and was the son of a miner. He was a poet, novelist and critic of society and is still a great influence. He tried to re-define the roles of men and women and mixed a wonderful visual imagination, with a quasi-mystical attitude to sex. His best novels are Sons and Lovers, *1913,* The Rainbow *(first published in 1915 and revised in 1926) and* Women in Love, *1921.*

Lawrence had T.B., and died in the South of France after travelling all over the world with his wife Frieda.

The Rainbow *is the story of two sisters, Ursula and Gudrun and their different attitudes to life and love.*

As Ursula passed from girlhood towards womanhood, gradually the cloud of self-responsibility gathered upon her. She became aware of herself, that she was a separate entity in the midst of an unseparated obscurity, that she must go somewhere, she must become something. And she was afraid, troubled. Why, or why must one grow up, why must one inherit this heavy, numbing responsibility of living an undiscovered life? Out of the nothingness and the undifferentiated mass, to make something of herself! But what? In the obscurity and pathlessness to take a direction! But whither? How take even one step? And yet, how stand still? This was torment indeed, to inherit the responsibility of one's life.

The religion which had been another world for her, a glorious sort of play-world, where she lived, climbing the tree with the short-statured man, walking shakily on the sea like the disciple, breaking the bread into five thousand portions, like the Lord, giving a great picnic to five thousand people, now fell away from reality, and became a tale, a myth, an illusion, which, however much one might assert it to be true an historical fact, one knew was not true—at least, for this present-day life of ours. There could, within the limits of this life we know, be no Feeding of the Five Thousand. And the girl had come to the point where she held that that which one cannot experience in daily life is not true for oneself.

So, the old duality of life, wherein there had been a weekday world of people and trains and duties and reports, and besides that a Sunday world of absolute truth and living mystery, of walking upon the waters and being blinded by the face of the Lord, of following the pillar of cloud across the desert and watching the bush that crackled yet did not burn away, this old, unquestioned duality suddenly was found to be broken apart. The weekday world had triumphed over the Sunday world. The Sunday world was not real, or at least, not actual. And one lived by action.

Only the weekday world mattered. She herself, Ursula Brangwen, must know how to take the weekday life. Her body must be a weekday body, held in the world's estimate. Her soul must have a weekday value, known according to the world's knowledge. Well, then, there was a weekday life to live, of action and deeds. And so there was a necessity to choose one's action and one's deeds. One was responsible to the world for what one did.

Nay, one was more than responsible to the world. One was responsible to oneself. There was some puzzling, tormenting residue of the Sunday world within her, some persistent Sunday self, which insisted upon a relationship with the now shed-away vision world. How could one keep up a relationship with that which one denied? Her task was now to learn the week-day life.

How to act, that was the question? Whither to go, how to become oneself? One was not oneself, one was merely a half-stated question. How to become oneself, how to know the question and the answer of oneself, when one was merely an unfixed something-nothing, blowing about like the winds of heaven, undefined, unstated.

She turned to the visions, which had spoken far-off words that ran along the blood like ripples of an unseen wind, she heard the words again, she denied the vision, for she must be a weekday person, to whom visions were not true, and she demanded only the weekday meaning of the words.

There were words spoken by the vision: and words must have a weekday meaning, since words were weekday stuff. Let them speak now: let them bespeak themselves in weekday terms. The vision should translate itself into weekday terms.

6 Wanting a Chance in Life

From *The Story of an African Farm*

by Olive Schreiner

Olive Schreiner (1855–1920) was born in South Africa, came to England when she was twenty-six and published under a male pseudonym. The Story of an African Farm, *a novel, was published in 1883 and was followed by* Women and Labour *in 1911. She was an ardent feminist.*

'They say women have one great and noble work left them, and they do it ill.—That is true; they do it execrably. It is the work that demands the broadest culture, and they have not even the narrowest. The lawyer may see no deeper than his law books, and the chemist see no further than the windows of his laboratory, and they may do their work well. But the woman who does woman's work needs a many-sided, multiform culture; the heights and depths of human life must not be beyond the reach of her vision; she must have knowledge of men and things in many states, a wide catholicity of sympathy, the strength that springs from knowledge, and the magnanimity which springs from strength. We bear the world, and we make it. The souls of little children are marvellously delicate and tender things, and keep for ever the shadow that first falls on them and, that is the mother's or at best a woman's. There was never a great man who had not a great mother—it is hardly an exaggeration. The first six years of our life make us; all that is added later is veneer; and yet some say, if a woman can cook a dinner or dress herself well she has culture enough.

'The mightiest and noblest of human work is given to us, and we do it ill. Send a navvy to work into an artist's studio, and see what you will find there! And yet, thank

God, we have this work,' she added quickly: 'it is the one window through which we see into the great world of earnest labour. The meanest girl who dances and dresses becomes something higher when her children look up into her face and ask her questions. It is the only education we have and which they cannot take from us.'

She smiled slightly. 'They say that we complain of woman's being compelled to look upon marriage as a profession; but that she is free to enter upon it or leave it as she pleases.

'Yes—and a cat set afloat in a pond is free to sit in the tub till it dies there, it is under no obligation to wet its feet; and a drowning man may catch at a straw or not, just as he likes—it is a glorious liberty! Let any man think for five minutes of what old maiden-hood means to a woman —and then let him be silent. Is it easy to bear through life a name that in itself signifies defeat? to dwell, as nine out of ten unmarried women must, under the finger of another woman? Is it easy to look forward to an old age without honour, without the reward of useful labour, without love?

7 Wanting Something More

From *Jane Eyre*

by Charlotte Brontë

Charlotte Brontë (1816–1855) was the eldest surviving daughter of a family of six, living at Haworth, Yorkshire, where her father was curate. She taught in a school for three years and was subsequently a governess. In 1842 she went with her sister Emily to study languages at a school in Brussels (cf. Villette *1853). Her other novels are* The Professor, *(published posthumously in 1857),* Jane Eyre, *1847 and* Shirley, *1849. She died after her brother and sisters in 1855 a few months after her marriage to her father's curate.* Jane Eyre *is the most popular of her novels and is basically a 'Cinderella' story. Charlotte Brontë was much concerned with the hopes and loves of women and although not as great a poet as her sister Emily, had both originality and passion. In the following extract Jane is a governess at Thornfield Hall, Mr. Rochester's house.*

Anybody may blame me who likes when I add further that now and then, when I took a walk by myself in the grounds, when I went down to the gates and looked through them along the road, or when, while Adele played with her nurse, and Mrs. Fairfax made jellies in the store-room, I climbed the three staircases, raised the trap-door to the attic, and having reached the leads, looked out afar over sequestered field and hill, and along dim sky-line—that then I longed for a power of vision which might overpass that limit; which might reach the busy world, towns, regions full of life I had heard of but never seen; that then I desired more of practical experience than I possessed; more of intercourse with my kind, of acquaintance with variety of character, than was here within my reach. I valued what was good in Mrs. Fairfax, and what was good in Adele; but I believed in the existence of other and more vivid kinds of goodness, and what I believed in I wish to behold.

Who blames me? Many, no doubt; and I shall be called discontented. I could not help it: the restlessness was in my nature; it agitated me to pain sometimes. Then my sole relief was to walk along the corridor of the third storey, backwards and forwards, safe in the silence and solitude of the spot and allow my mind's eye to dwell on whatever bright visions rose before it—and, certainly they were many and glowing; to let my heart be heard by the exultant movement, which, while it swelled it in trouble, expanded it with life; and, best of all, to open my inward ear to a tale that was never ended—a tale my imagination created, and narrated continuously; quickened with all of incident, life, fire, feeling, that I desired and had not in my actual existence.

It is in vain to say human beings ought to be satisfied with tranquillity: they must have action; and they will make it if they cannot find it. Millions are condemned to a stiller doom than mine, and millions are in silent revolt against their lot. Nobody knows how many rebellions besides political rebellions ferment in the masses of life which people earth. Women are supposed to be very calm generally but women feel just as men feel; they need exercise for their faculties and a field for their efforts as much as their brothers do; they suffer from too rigid a restraint, too absolute a stagnation, precisely as men would suffer; and it is narrow-minded in their more privileged fellow-creatures to say that they ought to confine themselves to making puddings and knitting stockings, to playing on the piano and embroidering bags. It is thoughtless to condemn them, or laugh at them, if they seek to do more or learn more than custom has pronounced necessary for their sex.

8 A Young Girl's Aspirations

From *Journals*

by Marie Bashkirtseff

Marie Bashkirtseff (1859–1884) was born in Russia and lived the life of an emigrée with her family in France. She was a precocious child who wished to become a painter and studied for this in Paris. She died young of T.B. Her Journal *was published posthumously, selected by her mother. (The complete diaries are to be found in the Bibliothèque Nationale in Paris). The story of her infatuation with the Duke of Hamilton has just been written by Doris Langley Moore. Her* Letters *have also been published. Marie is memorable chiefly because of the rapturous ardour with which she confronts life, mixed with conceit and self-infatuation. She was a remarkable if not very likeable girl.*

Sunday, July 2nd 1876.

Oh, how hot it is! and how dull. No, I am wrong in calling it dull; one cannot be dull with so many mental resources as I have. I am not dull, because I can read, sing, paint, and muse to myself, but I am restless and depressed.

Is my poor youth to be spent between the dining-room and petty domestic worries? A woman lives from sixteen to forty. I shudder at the thought of losing even a month of my life.

What is the good of having studied, of having tried to know more than other women, of priding myself on knowing all the branches of learning that are attributed to famous men in their biographies?

I have some idea of them all, but I have only really gone

into history, literature and natural philosophy, so as to read everything about them—everything that is interesting. As a matter of fact, I find everything interesting that I put my heart into, and this sets me on fire.

What then is the good of my having studied and thought? Why endowed with wit, beauty, and a voice? To grow mouldy, to be bored to death? If I were ignorant and coarse, perhaps I should be happy.

Not a single living soul to talk to! A girl of sixteen cannot be quite satisfied with the family circle, especially when she is a girl like me.

Of course grandpa is clever. But then he is old and blind, and he is everlastingly quarrelling with his man Triphon and grumbling about the dinner.

Mamma has plenty of *esprit* but not much information; her manners are not polished, she hasn't any tact, and her mind has got dull and rusty, through her never talking about anything but the servants, my health and the dogs.

Auntie is rather better. She even rather impresses you when you don't know her well.

Have I ever mentioned their ages? Mamma would still be a fine woman if it were not for her bad health. Auntie is a few years younger, but she looks the elder of the two. She is not good-looking, but tall and well proportioned.

**Amor decrescit ubique crescere non possit.*

That is why lovers, when once they have felt perfectly happy, begin imperceptibly to love each other less and less, and end at last by drifting apart altogether.

I am going away tomorrow. I can't say how sorry I am to leave Nice.

All these preparations for the journey rather damp my resolution.

I have selected the music to take with me, and some books, the encyclopaedia, a volume each of Plato, Dante, Ariosto and Shakespeare; also a number of English novels by Bulmer, Collins and Dickens.

I was rude to auntie, and then I went out on the terrace. I stopped out in the garden till dusk. How lovely the twi-

---

* It is *dolar* in Syons but I say *Amor* because the maxim is equally applicable to both. (M.B.)

light is with the sea and space for background, and these luxuriant plants and thick foliaged trees! And then, by way of contrast, the bamboos and palm-trees. The fountain, the grotto with its little waterfall trickling from rock to rock before falling into the basin. All round, the bushy trees give the spot a look of peacefulness and mystery, which makes me lazy and sets me dreaming.

Why does water always make me dreamy?

I stopped in the garden and looked at a stone vase in which a lovely canna rose was just unfolding. I thought how pretty my white dress and leafy crown must look in that entrancing garden.

Is *that* all I am ever to do in life—dress myself carefully, put leaves in my hair, and think about the effect.

Well, candidly, if other people were to read me I think they would consider me a bore. I am still so young, I know so little of life!

I cannot speak with the authority or the assurance of writers who profess—what presumption!—to know men, to lay down laws and to bind their maxims on other people.

My maid is here with a dress for me to wear tomorrow; it reminds me of my departure.

9 Being Non-Educated

From *Letters*

by Mary Kingsley

Mary Kingsley (1862–1900) was a traveller and the niece of the novelist Charles Kingsley. After her parents' death when she was thirty she went alone to West Africa in order to complete a work on native religion and law which her father, an explorer, had not been able to finish. She made many valuable observations. The impression of her, a Victorian spinster alone except for her umbrella in 'Darkest Africa' is formidable. Nowadays she would probably be a Professor of Anthropology. Her book Travels in West Africa, *1897, is extremely original and unbiased. She died nursing prisoners at Simon's Town during the Boer War*

The whole of my childhood and youth was spent at home, in the house and garden. The living outside world I saw little of, and cared less for, for I felt myself out of place at the few parties I ever had the chance of going to, and I deservedly was unpopular with my own generation, for I knew nothing of play and such things. But this was not superiority of mind in me, at all; the truth was I had a great amusing world of my own other people did not know, or care about—that was in the books in my father's library.

They were mostly old books on the West Indies, and old medical books, and old travel books and what not; fiction was represented in it by the works of Smollett, and little else. No-one would believe the number, or character, of the books I absorbed. I did not say anything about them, finding if I did it generally meant an injunction not to do it. My favourites among them were Burton's *Anatomy of Melancholy*, Johnson's *Robberies and Murders of the Most*

Notorious Pirates and Bayle's *Dictionary*. When my father was home from one of his long and many journeys, new books used to come into the house, and although I did not like them as the old, yet they had to be read too. But just as I was coming to the conclusion that new books were unworthy of my serious attention, one turned up that fascinated me wildly. It was *Solar Physics* by Professor Norman Lockyer. That book opened a new world for me, and also got me into trouble in my old one.

It was difficult to get hold of it because my father was interested in it too, but I still stuck to it, and one dreadful evening my father's friend, the doctor, came in. My father asked him if had read *Solar Physics* and said it was an interesting book, etc., and finally that he would lend it to him and send it round in the morning. I thought 'No, not if I know it will you lend that book,' and so I took it and hid it away in some straw in a shed.

I need not say when a search for it next morning was instituted I was held to know where it was. I said neither aye nor nay, and the book returned to civilised society when I had got right through it, not before.

About this time I developed a passionate devotion for the science of chemistry, and I went in for it—experiments not being allowed—in the available books in the library. Most of them were books on alchemy, and the rest entirely obsolete. After most carefully getting up all the information these could give me, I happened on a gentleman who knew modern chemistry, and tried my information on him. He said he had not heard anything so ridiculous for years, and recommended I should be placed in a museum as a compendium of exploded chemical theories, which hurt my feelings very much, and I cried bitterly at not being taught things.

My home authorities said I had no business to want to be taught such things, but presented me with a copy of Craik's *Pursuit of Knowledge Under Difficulties*. From this book I learned how man had invented the steam engine from observing the habits of tea-kettles, and mastered exceedingly difficult dead languages from merely finding a leaf of a book, written therein, in a dust-bin, and subsequently had attained such eminence in their respective walks of knowledge that Europe trembled at their name. This lesson went home. I saw it was silly to go whining about looking for someone to teach me; if I wanted scientific knowledge there were kettles, and in addition, an extremely complicated pump which was always out of order, while if I wanted scholarship there was the library to go on with, with the addition of my brother's school-books.

I worked very hard in a time-wasting way at mathematics, seeing I must know something of them for science, and I got enough money to take in that delightful paper *The English Mechanic*. What *The English Mechanic* was to me for years I cannot explain. What I should have done without its companionship between sixteen and twenty I do not care to think. We had at this period of my existence moved down into north-west Kent, to a secluded spot where the houses were always in some state of dilapidation, where the residents had to be handy-men if they would not lead miserable existences. With the aid of *The English Mechanic* I became a handy man. During the early stages of my education, I used up a good deal of rag one way and another, and shed a deal of gore of my own. But I got on.

One of my greatest trials was connected with plumbing work. I met with a crisis before I was equal to it. A pipe required cutting off in the coach-house. The affair was urgent; it required very little to bring a ceiling down in that locality at any time, and upstairs water was soaking into one freely. The pipe which was doing it presented itself freely in the coach-house below, and if I could cut it through and double it back, and hammer it up neatly all would be well. We had a boy connected with odd jobs too, then and I summoned him to attend on me and my operations. He was impressed with the workmanlike manner in which I proceeded. Standing on a box I cut the lead pipe gallantly through; swish came out a jet of water that knocked me over, box and all, and played on me as if I were a rick-fire and it was the local fire-brigade, and a wild yell of joy came from that wretched boy. Of course I ought to have turned the water off from the main, and so on, first, but, as I have said, my education was unfinished in *plumbing* at the time.

'I don't know if I ever revealed the fact to you that being allowed to learn German was *all* the paid-for education I ever had. £2,000 was spent on my brother's, I still hope not in vain. The man who taught me German found I had worked myself up to a point by wrong methods but still there I was; and so he just took *Faust* and spelt it out with me, and I *am* it, and can say "Habe nun ach! Philosophie" etc. But here I and *Faust* part, for I want no Devil. I have gone off with the *Erdgeist*.'

* * *

After her mother's and father's death she wrote:

'And then, when the fight was lost, when there were no more odd jobs anyone wanted me to do at home, I, out of my life in books, found something to do that my father had cared for, something for which I had been taught German, so that I could do for him odd jobs in it.

It was the study of early religion and law, and for it I had to go to West Africa, and I went there, proceeding on the even tenour of my way, doing odd jobs and trying to understand things, pursuing knowledge under difficulties with unbroken devotion.'

10 Weak Woman

From *A Vindication of the Rights of Women*

by Mary Wollstonecraft

Mary Wollstonecraft (1759–1797) had been like Charlotte Brontë both a teacher and a governess. She was an ardent feminist and held emancipated and progressive views on most subjects. She had a love affair in Paris with Gilbert Imlay who was not worthy of her rare mixture of idealism, femininity and moral strength. They had a daughter, Fanny. In 1797 she married the famous political philosopher and man of ideas, William Godwin, after living with him for some time. She died after the birth of her daughter Mary who later married the poet Shelley. The Vindication of the Rights of Woman *was published in 1792 and is a most powerful and advanced piece of sustained polemic. The letters to Imlay were first edited in 1879 [see Extract No. 30].*

It would be an endless task to trace the variety of meannesses, cares, and sorrows, into which women are plunged by the prevailing opinion, that they were created rather to feel than reason, and that all the power they obtain, must be obtained by their charms and weakness:
'Fine by defect, and amiably weak!'
And, made by this amiable weakness entirely dependent, excepting what they gain by illicit sway, on man, not only for protection, but advice, is it surprising that, neglecting the duties that reason alone points out, and shrinking from trials calculated to strengthen their minds, they only exert themselves to give their defects a graceful covering, which may serve to heighten their charms in the eye of the volup-

tuary, though it sink them below the scale of moral existence.

Fragile in every sense of the word, they are obliged to look up to man for every comfort. In the most trifling dangers they cling to their support, with parasitical tenacity, piteously demanding succour; and their *natural* protector extends his arm or lifts up his voice, to guard the lovely trembler—from what? Perhaps the frown of an old cow, or the jump of a mouse; a rat would be a serious danger. In the name of reason, and even common sense, what can save such beings from contempt; even though they be soft and fair?

These fears, when not affected, may be very pretty; but they show a degree of imbecility that degrades a rational creature in a way women are not aware of—for love and esteem are very distinct things.

I am fully persuaded that we should hear of none of these infantine airs, if girls were allowed to take sufficient exercise and not confined in close rooms till their muscles are relaxed, and their powers of digestion destroyed. To carry the remark still further, if fear in girls, instead of being cherished, perhaps created, was treated in the same manner as cowardice in boys, we should quickly see women with more dignified aspects. It is true, they could not then with equal propriety be termed the sweet flowers that smile in the walk of man; but they would be more respectable members of society, and discharge the important duties of life by the light of their own reason. 'Educate women like men,' says Rousseau, 'and the more they resemble our sex the less power will they have over us.' This is the very point I aim at. I do not wish them to have power over men; but over themselves.

11 Being in Love I

From *Emma*

by Jane Austen

Jane Austen (1775–1817) lived the outward life of a middle-class spinster and her first novel Sense and Sensibility *did not appear till six years before her death, followed rapidly by* Pride and Prejudice, Mansfield Park, Emma, Northanger Abbey *and* Persuasion, *although early drafts were begun as early as 1795. Her* Letters *were first edited in 1932 and are primarily written to her sister, Cassandra, in a gossipy vein. Even here her clear, astringent style reminds us of the wit of the novels.*

Emma *is the story of Emma Woodhouse whose attempts to influence the life of young Harriet Smith almost end in disaster for them both. The novel charts the self-discovery of the heroine.*

Emma continued to entertain no doubt of her being in love. Her ideas only varied as to the how much. At first she thought it was a good deal; and afterwards but little. She had great pleasure in hearing Frank Churchill talked of; and, for his sake, greater pleasure than ever in seeing Mr. and Mrs. Weston; she was very often thinking of him, and quite impatient for a letter, that she might know how he was, how were his spirits, how was his aunt, and what was the chance of his coming to Randalls again this spring. But, on the other hand, she could not admit herself to be unhappy, nor, after the first morning, to be less disposed for employment than usual; she was still busy and cheerful; and, pleasing as he was, she could yet imagine him to have faults; and further, though thinking of him so much, and, as she sat drawing or working, forming a thousand amusing schemes for the progress and close of their attachment, fancying interesting dialogues, and inventing elegant letters; the conclusion of every imaginary declaration on his side was that she *refused him*. Their affection was always to subside into friendship. Everything tender and charming was to mark their parting; but still they were to part. When she became sensible of this, it struck her that she could not be very much in love; for, in spite of her previous and fixed determination never to quit her father, never to marry, a strong attachment certainly must produce more of a struggle than she could foresee in her own feelings.

'I do not find myself making any use of the word *sacrifice*,' said she. 'In not one of all my clever replies, my delicate negatives, is there any allusion to making a sacrifice. I do suspect that he is not really necessary to my happiness. So much the better. I certainly will not persuade myself to feel more than I do. I am quite enough in love. I should be sorry to be more.'

Upon the whole, she was equally contented with her view of his feelings.

'*He* is undoubtedly very much in love—everything denotes it—very much in love indeed!—and when he comes again, if his affection continue, I must be on my guard not to encourage it. It would be most inexcusable to do otherwise, as my own mind is quite made up. Not that I imagine he can think I have been encouraging him hitherto. No; if he had believed me at all to share his feelings he would not have been so wretched. Could he have thought himself encouraged, his looks and language at parting would have been different. Still, however, I must be on my guard. This in the supposition of his attachment continuing what it now is; but I do not know that I expect it will; I do not look upon him to be quite the sort of man—I do not altogether build upon his steadiness or constancy. His feelings are warm, but I can imagine them rather changeable. Every consideration of the subject, in short, makes me thankful that my happiness is not more deeply involved. I shall do very well again after a little while—and then, it will be a good thing over; for they say everybody is in love once in their lives, and I shall have been let off easily.'

12 Planning for the Future

From *Middlemarch*

by George Eliot

George Eliot was the pen-name of Mary Ann Evans who was born in Warwickshire in 1819. She was much interested in theology but it was not till after her common law marriage with G. H. Lewes that she published novels. Adam Bede, *1859, and* The Mill on the Floss, *1860, were followed by many others including* Middlemarch, *1871–2, which was first published in instalments and is regarded by many modern critics as her most successful and profound work. She died in 1880.*

Middlemarch *is set in the English provinces in the early years of the nineteenth century. Two women are contrasted in it—the ardent Dorothea and the beautiful but more ordinary Rosamond and the story of their marriages is unfolded. [See also No. 32.]*

And how should Dorothea not marry?—a girl so handsome and with such prospects? Nothing could hinder it but her love of extremes, and her insistence on regulating life according to notions which might cause a wary man to hesitate before he made her an offer, or even might lead her at last to refuse all offers. A young lady of some birth and fortune, who knelt suddenly down on a brick floor by the side of a sick labourer and prayed fervidly as if she thought herself living in the time of the Apostles—who had strange whims of fasting like a Papist, and of sitting up at night to read old theological books! Such a wife might awaken you some fine morning with a new scheme for the application of her income which would interfere with political economy and the keeping of saddle-horses:

a man would naturally think twice before he risked himself in such fellowship. Women were expected to have weak opinions; but the great safeguard of society and of domestic life was, that opinions were not acted on. Sane people did what their neighbours did, so that if any lunatics were at large, one might know and avoid them.

The rural opinion about the new young ladies, even among the cottagers, was generally in favour of Celia, as being so amiable and innocent-looking, while Miss Brooke's large eyes seemed, like her religion, too unusual and striking. Poor Dorothea! compared with her, the innocent-looking Celia was knowing and worldly-wise; so much subtler is a human mind than the outside tissues which make a sort of blazonry or clock-face for it.

Yet those who approached Dorothea, though prejudiced against her by this alarming hearsay, found that she had a charm unaccountably reconcilable with it. Most men thought her bewitching when she was on horseback. She loved the fresh air and the various aspects of the country, and when her eyes and cheeks glowed with mingled pleasure she looked very little like a devotee. Riding was an indulgence which she allowed herself in spite of conscientious qualms; she felt that she enjoyed it in a pagan sensuous way, and always looked forward to renouncing it.

She was open, ardent, and not in the least self-admiring; indeed, it was pretty to see how her imagination adorned her sister Celia with attractions altogether superior to her own, and if any gentleman appeared to come to the Grange from some other motive than that of seeing Mr. Brooke, she concluded that he must be in love with Celia: Sir James Chettam, for example, whom she constantly considered from Celia's point of view, inwardly debating whether it would be good for Celia to accept him. That he should be regarded as a suitor to herself would have seemed to her a ridiculous irrelevance. Dorothea, with all her eagerness to know the truths of life, retained very childlike ideas about marriage. She felt sure that she would have accepted the judicious Hooker, if she had been born in time to save him from that wretched mistake he made in matrimony; or John Milton when his blindness had come on; or any of the other great men whose odd habits it would have been glorious piety to endure; but an amiable handsome baronet, who said 'Exactly' to her remarks even when she expressed uncertainty,—how could he affect her as a lover? The really delightful marriage must be that where your husband was a sort of father, and could teach you even Hebrew, if you wished it.

13 Being a Governess

From *Agnes Grey*

by Anne Brontë

Anne Brontë (1820–1849) was the youngest of the Brontë sisters and wrote both poems and novels. Agnes Grey *was published in 1847 and* The Tenant of Wildfell Hall *a year later. She died of tuberculosis.*

Anne was also a governess and Agnes Grey *is semi-autobiographical.*

My task of instruction and surveillance, instead of becoming easier as my charges and I got better accustomed to each other, became more arduous as their characters unfolded. The name of governess, I soon found, was a mere mockery as applied to me, my pupils had no more notion of obedience than a wild unbroken colt.

The habitual fear of their father's peevish temper, and the dread of the punishments he was wont to inflict when irritated, kept them generally within bounds in his immediate presence. The girls, too, had some fear of their mother's anger, and the boy might occasionally be bribed to do as she bid him by the hope of reward: but I had no rewards to offer, and as for punishments, I was given to understand, the parents reserved that privilege to themselves; and yet they expected me to keep my pupils in order. Other children might be guided by the fear of anger, and the desire of approbation; but neither the one nor the other had any effect upon these.

Master Tom, not content with refusing to be ruled, must needs set up as a ruler, and manifested a determination to keep, not only his sisters, but his governess in order, by violent manual and pedal applications; and, as he was a tall, strong boy of his years, this occasioned no trifling inconvenience.

A few sound boxes on the ear, on such occasions, might have settled the matter easily enough: but as, in that case, he might make up some story to his mother, which she would be sure to believe, as she had such unshaken faith in his veracity—though I had already discovered it to be by no means unimpeachable—I determined to refrain from striking him, even in self-defence: and, in his most violent moods, my only resources was to throw him on his back, and hold his hands and feet until the frenzy was somewhat abated.

To the difficulty of preventing him from doing what he ought not, was added that of forcing him to do what he ought. Often he would positively refuse to learn, or to repeat his lessons, or even to look at his book. Here, again, a good birch rod might have been serviceable: but as my powers were so limited, I must make the best use of what I had.

As there were no settled hours for study and play, I resolved to give my pupils a certain task, which, with moderate attention, they could perform in a short time; and till this was done, however weary I was, or however perverse they might be, nothing short of parental interference should induce me to suffer them to leave the schoolroom; even if I should sit with my chair against the door to keep them in. Patience, Firmness and Perseverance were my only weapons; and these I resolved to use to the utmost.

I determined always strictly to fulfil the threats and promises I made; and, to that end, I must be cautious to threaten and promise nothing that I could not perform. Then, I would carefully refrain from all useless irritability and indulgence of my own ill-temper: when they behaved tolerably, I would be as kind and obliging as it was in my power to be, in order to make the widest possible distinction between their good and bad conduct; I would reason with them, too, in the simplest and most effective manner. When I reproved them, or refused to gratify their wishes, after a glaring fault, it should be more in sorrow than in anger: their little hymns and prayers I would make plain and clear to their understanding; when they said their prayers at night, and asked pardon for their offences, I would remind them of the sins of the past day, solemnly, but in perfect kindness, to avoid raising a spirit of opposition: penitential hymns should be said by the naughty; cheerful ones by the comparatively good: and every possible kind of instruction I would convey to them, as much as possible by entertaining discourse—apparently with no other object than their present amusement in view.

By these means I hoped, in time, both to benefit the children and to gain the approbation of their parents; and also to convince my friends at home that I was not so wanting in skill and prudence as they supposed. I knew the difficulties I had to contend with were great; but I knew (at least I believed) unremitting patience and perseverance could overcome them; and night and morning I implored Divine assistance to this end. But either the children were so incorrigible, the parents so unreasonable or myself so mistaken in my views, or so unable to carry them out, that my best intentions and most strenuous efforts seemed productive of no better result than sport to the children, dissatisfactions to their parents, and torment to myself.

The task of instruction was as arduous for the body as for the mind. I had to run after my pupils to catch them, to carry or drag them to the table, and often forcibly to hold them there till the lesson was done. Tom I frequently put into a corner, seating myself before him in a chair, with a book which contained the little task that must be said or read, before he was released, in my hand. He was not strong enough to push both me and the chair away, so he would stand twisting his body and face into the most grotesque and singular contortions—laughable, no doubt, to an unconcerned spectator, but not to me—and uttering loud yells and doleful oratories, intended to represent weeping, but wholly without the accompaniment of tears. I knew this was done solely for the purpose of annoying me; and, therefore, however I might inwardly tremble with impatience and irritation, I manfully strove to suppress all visible signs of molestation, and affected to sit with calm indifference, waiting till it should please him to cease this pastime, and prepare for a run in the garden, by casting his eye on the book and reading or repeating the few words he was required to say.

Sometimes he would determine to do his writing badly: and I had to hold his hand to prevent him from purposely blotting or disfiguring the paper. Frequently I threatened that, if he did not do better, he should have another line; then he would stubbornly refuse to write this line, and I, to save my word, had finally to restort to the expedient of holding his fingers upon the pen, and forcibly drawing his hand up and down, till, in spite of his resistance, the line was in some sort completed.

Yet Tom was by no means the most unmanageable of my pupils: sometimes, to my great joy, he would have the sense to see that his wisest policy was to finish his tasks, and go out and amuse himself till I and his sisters came to join him; which frequently was not at all, for Mary Ann seldom followed his example in this particular: she apparently preferred rolling on the floor to any other amusement. Down she would drop like a leaden weight; and when I, with great difficulty had succeeded in rooting her thence, I had still to hold her up with one arm, while with the other I held the book from which she was to read or spell her lesson. As the dead weight of the big girl of six became too heavy for one arm to bear, I transferred it to the other; or, if both were weary of the burden, I carried her into a corner, and told her she might come out when she should find the use of her feet, and stand up; but she generally preferred lying there like a log till dinner or tea time, when, as I could not deprive her of her meals, she must be liberated, and would come crawling out with a grin of triumph on her round, red face.

Often she would stubbornly refuse to pronounce some particular word in her lesson, and now I regret the lost labour I have had in striving to conquer her obstinacy. If I had passed it over as a matter of no consequence it would have been better for both parties, than vainly striving to overcome it as I did, but I thought it my absolute duty to crush this vicious tendency in the bud, and so it was, if I could have done it, and had my powers been less limited,

I might have enforced obedience; but, as it was, it was a trial of strength between her and me, in which she generally came off victorious; and every victory served to encourage and strengthen her for a future contest.

In vain I argued, coaxed, entreated, threatened, scolded; in vain I kept her in from play, or, if obliged to take her out, refused to play with her, or to speak kindly, or have anything to do with her; in vain I tried to set before her the advantages of doing as she was bid, and being loved and kindly treated in consequence, and the disadvantages of persisting in her absurd perversity. Sometimes when she would ask me to do something for her, I would answer—

'Yes, I will, Mary Ann, if you will only say that word. Come! You'd better say it at once, and have no more trouble about it.'

'No.'

'Then, of course, I can do nothing for you.'

With me, at her age, or under, neglect and disgrace were the most dreadful punishments: but on her they made no impression.

Sometimes, exasperated to the utmost pitch, I would shake her violently by the shoulder, or pull her long hair, or put her in the corner; for which she punished me with loud, shrill, piercing screams, that went through my head like a knife. She knew I hated this, and when she had shrieked her utmost, would look into my face with an air of vindictive satisfaction, exclaiming—

'*Now*, then! *that's* for you.'

And then shriek again and again, till I was forced to stop my ears. Often these dreadful cries would bring Mrs. Bloomfield up to enquire what was the matter?

'Mary Ann is a naughty girl, ma'am.'

'But what are these shocking screams?'

'She is screaming in a passion.'

'I never heard such a dreadful noise! You might be killing her. Why is she not with her brother?'

'I cannot get her to finish her lessons.'

'But Mary Ann must be a *good* girl and finish her lessons.' This was blandly spoken to the child.

'And I hope I shall *never* hear such terrible cries again!'

And fixing her cold stony eyes on me with a look that could not be mistaken, she would shut the door, and walk away.

Sometimes I would try to take the little obstinate creature by surprise, and casually ask her the word whilst she was thinking of something else, frequently she would begin to say it, and then suddenly check herself, with a provoking look that seemed to say, 'Ah! I'm too sharp for you; you shan't trick it out of me, either.'

On another occasion, I pretended to forget the whole affair; and talked and played with her as usual, till night, when I put her to bed; then bending over her, while she lay all smiles and good humour, just before departing, I said, as cheerfully and kindly as before—

'Now, Mary Ann, just tell me that word before I kiss you goodnight: you are a good girl now, and of course you will say it.'

'No, I won't.'

'Then I can't kiss you.'

'Well, I don't care.'

In vain I expressed my sorrow; in vain I lingered for some symptom of contrition; she really 'didn't care', and I left her alone, and in darkness, wondering most of all at this last proof of insensate stubbornness. In *my* childhood, I could not imagine a more afflictive punishment than for my mother to refuse to kiss me at night: the very idea was terrible. More than the idea I never felt, for, happily I never committed a crime that was deemed worthy of such a penalty; but once I remember, for some transgression of my sister's, our mother thought proper to inflict it upon her: what *she* felt, I cannot tell; but my sympathetic tears and suffering for her sake, I shall not soon forget.

Another troublesome trait in Mary Ann, was her incorrigible propensity to keep running into the nursery, to play with her little sisters and the nurse. This was natural enough, but, as it was against her mother's express desire, I, of course, forbade her to do so, and did my utmost to keep her with me: but that only increased her relish for the nursery, and the more I strove to keep her out of it, the oftener she went, and the longer she stayed—to the great dissatisfaction of Mrs. Bloomfield, who, I well knew, would impute all the blame of the matter to me.

Another of my trials was the dressing in the morning: at one time she would not be washed; at another she would not be dressed, unless she might wear some particular frock, that I knew her mother would not like her to have; at another she would scream and run away if I attempted to touch her hair. So that, frequently, when after much trouble and toil, I had, at length, succeeded in bringing her down, the breakfast was nearly half over; and black looks from 'mamma', and testy observations from 'papa', spoken at me, if not to me, were sure to be my need; for few things irritated the latter so much as want of punctuality at meal times.

Then, among the minor annoyances, was my inability to satisfy Mrs. Bloomfield with her daughter's dress; and the child's hair 'was never fit to be seen.' Sometimes, as a powerful reproach to me, she would perform the office of tirewoman herself, and then complain bitterly of the trouble it gave her.

When little Fanny came into the schoolroom, I hoped she would be mild and inoffensive, at least; but a few days, if not a few hours, sufficed to destroy the illusion: I found her a mischievous, intractable little creature, given up to falsehood and deception, young as she was, and alarmingly fond of exercising her two favourite weapons of offence and defence: that of spitting in the faces of those who incurred her displeasure, and bellowing like a bull when her unreasonable desires were not gratified. As she, generally, was pretty quiet in her parents' presence, and they were impressed with the notion of her being a remarkably gentle child, her falsehoods were readily believed, and her loud uproars led them to suspect harsh and injudicious treatment on my part; and when, at length, her bad disposition became manifest even to their prejudiced eyes, I felt that the whole was attributed to me.

'What a naughty girl Fanny is getting!' Mrs. Bloomfield would say to her spouse. 'Don't you observe, my dear, how she is altered since she entered the schoolroom? She will soon be as bad as the other two; and, I am sorry to say, they have quite deteriorated of late.'

'You may say that,' was the answer. 'I've been thinking that same myself. I thought when we got them a governess they'd improve; but, instead of that, they get worse and worse: I don't know how it is with their learning; but their habits, I know, make no sort of improvement; they get rougher and dirtier, and more unseemly every day.'

I knew this was pointed at me; and these and all similar innuendoes, affected me far more deeply than any open accusations would have done; for against the latter I should have been roused to speak in my own defence; now I judged it my wisest plan to subdue every resentful impulse, suppress every sensitive shrinking, and go on perseveringly, doing my best; for, irksome as my situation was, I earnestly wished to retain it. I thought, if I could struggle on with unremitting firmness and integrity, the children would in time become more humanized: every month would contribute to make them some little wiser, and, consequently, more manageable; for a child of nine or ten as frantic and ungovernable as these at six and seven would be a maniac.

I flattered myself I was benefiting my parents and sister by my continuance here; for, small as the salary was, I still was earning something, and with strict economy I could easily manage to have something to spare for them, if they would favour me by taking it. Then it was by my own will that I had got the place: I had brought all this tribulation on myself, and I was determined to bear it; nay, more than that, I did not even regret the step I had taken. I longed to show my friends that, even now, I was competent to undertake the charge, and able to acquire myself honourably to the end; and if ever I felt it degrading to submit so quietly, or intolerable to toil so constantly, I would turn towards my house, and say within myself—

'They may crush, but they shall not subdue me

'Tis of thee that I think, not of them.'

About Christmas I was allowed to visit home; but my holiday was only of a fortnight's duration.

'For,' said Mrs. Bloomfield, 'I thought, as you had seen

your friends so lately, you would not care for a longer stay.' I left her to think so still: but she little knew how long, how wearisome those fourteen weeks of absence had been to me; how intensely I had longed for my holidays, how greatly I was disappointed at their curtailment. Yet she was not to blame in this; I had never told her my feelings, and she could not be expected to divine them; I had not been with her a full term, and she was justified in not allowing me a full vacation.

14 Being Engaged

From *The Egoist*

by George Meredith

George Meredith (1828–1909) was a journalist, poet and novelist. He married the widowed daughter of Peacock (see extract No. 40). His greatest novels were The Ordeals of Richard Feverel, *1859*, The Egoist, *1879*, The Tragic Comedians, *1880, and* Diana of the Crossways, *1885. His heroines are usually very spirited girls, perhaps rather far removed from the prevailing ideal of his own century.*
  The Egoist *is the story of Clara Middleton who is engaged to the conceited Sir Willoughby Patterne and has some trouble struggling free.*

In other words, love is an affair of two, and is only for two that can be as quick, as constant in intercommunication as are sun and earth, through the cloud or face to face. They take their breath of life from one another in signs of affection, proofs of faithfulness, incentives to admiration. Thus it is with men and women in love's good season. But a solitary soul dragging a log, must make the log a God to rejoice in the burden. That is not love.
  Clara was the least fitted of all women to drag a log. Few girls would be so rapid in exhausting capital. She was feminine indeed, but she wanted comradeship, a living and frank exchange of the best in both, with the deeper feelings untroubled. To be fixed at the mouth of a mine, and to have to descend it daily, and not to discover great opulence below; on the contrary, to be chilled in subterranean sunlessness, without any substantial quality that she could grasp, only the mystery of inefficient tallow-light in those caverns of the complacent talking man: this appeared to her too

extreme a probation for two or three weeks. How of a lifetime of it!

She was compelled by her nature to hope, expect, and believe that Sir Willoughby would again be the man she had known when she accepted him. Very singularly, to show her simple spirit at the time, she was unaware of any physical coldness to him; she knew of nothing but her mind at work, objecting to this and that, desiring changes. She did not dream of being on the giddy ridge of the passive or negative sentiment of love, where one step to the wrong side precipitates us into the state of repulsion.

Her eyes were lively at their meeting—so were his. She liked to see him on the steps, with young Crossjay under his arm. Sir Willoughby told her in his pleasantest humour of the boy's having got into the laboratory that morning to escape his taskmaster, and blown out the windows. She administered a chiding to the delinquent in the same spirit, while Sir Willoughby led her on his arm across the threshold, whispering, 'Soon for good!' In reply to the whisper, she begged for more of the story of young Crossjay. 'Come into the laboratory,' said he, a little less laughingly than softly; and Clara begged her father to come and see young Crossjay's latest pranks. Sir Willoughby whispered to her of the length of their separation and his joy to welcome her to the house where she would rein as mistress *very* soon. He numbered the weeks. He whispered, 'Come.' In the hurry of the moment she did not examine a lightning terror that shot through her. It passed, and was no more than the shadow which bends the summer grasses, leaving a ruffle of her ideas, in wonder of her having feared herself for something. Her father was with them. She and Willoughby were not yet alone.

Young Crossjay had not accomplished so fine a piece of destruction as Sir Willoughby's humour proclaimed of him. He had connected a battery with a train of gunpowder, shattering a window-frame and unsettling some bricks. Dr. Middleton asked if the youth was excluded from the library, and rejoiced to hear that it was a sealed door to him. Thither they went. Vernon Whitford was away on one of his long walks.

'There, papa, you see he is not so very faithful to you,' said Clara.

Dr. Middleton stood frowning over MS. notes on the table, in Vernon's handwriting. He flung up the hair from his forehead and dropped into a seat to inspect them closely. He was now immoveable. Clara was obliged to leave him there. She was led to think that Willoughby had drawn them to the library with the design to be rid of her protector, and she began to fear him. She proposed to pay her respects to the ladies Eleanor and Isabel. They were not seen, and a footman reported in the drawing-room that they were out driving. She grasped young Crossjay's hand. Sir Willoughby despatched him to Mrs. Montague, the housekeeper, for a tea of cakes and jam.

'Off!' he said, and the boy had to run.

Clara saw herself without a shield.

'And the garden!' she cried. 'I love the garden; I must go and see what flowers are up with you. In Spring I care most for wild flowers, and if you will show me daffodils, and crocuses, and anemones. . . .'

'My dearest Clara! my bride!' said he.

'Because they are vulgar flowers?' she asked him artlessly, to account for his detaining her.

Why would he not wait to deserve her!—no, not deserve —to reconcile her with her real position; not reconcile, but to repair the image of him in her mind, before he claimed his apparent right!

He did not wait. He pressed her to his bosom.

'You are mine, my Clara—utterly mine; every thought, every feeling. We are one: the world may do its worst. I have been longing for you, looking forward. You save me from a thousand vexations. One is perpetually crossed. That is all outside us. We too! With you I am secure. Soon! I could not tell you whether the world's alive or dead. My dearest!'

She came out of it with the sensations of the frightened child that has had its dip in sea-water, thankful to her ordeal for being over. And, after all, it was not so severe a trial. Such was her idea; and she said to herself immediately: What am I that I should complain? Two minutes earlier she would not have thought it; but humiliated pride falls lower than humbleness.

She did not blame him; she fell in her own esteem; less because she was the betrothed Clara Middleton, which was now palpable as a shot in the breast of a bird, than that she was a captured woman, of whom it is absolutely expected that she must submit, and when she would rather be gazing at flowers. Clara had shame of her sex. They cannot take a step without becoming bondswomen; into what a slavery! For herself, her trial was over, she thought. As for herself, she merely complained of a prematureness and crudity best unanalysed. In truth, she could hardly be said to complain. She did but criticise him and wonder that a man was unable to perceive, or was not arrested by perceiving, unwillingness, discordance, dull compliance; the bondwoman's due instead of the bride's consent. Oh, sharp distinction, as between two spheres!

She meted him justice; she admitted that he had spoken in a lover-like tone. Had it not been for the iteration of 'the world,' she would not have objected critically to his words, though they were words of downright appropriation. He had the right to use them, since she was to be married to him. But if he had only waited before playing the privileged lover!

Sir Willoughby was enraptured with her. Even so purely, coldly, statue-like, Dian-like, would he have prescribed his bride's reception of his caress. The suffusion of crimson coming over her subsequently, showing her divinely feminine in reflective bashfulness, agreed with his highest definitions of female character.

'Let me conduct you to the garden, my love,' he said.

She replied, 'I think I would rather go to my room.'

'I will send you a wild-flower posy.'

'Flowers, no; I do not like them to be gathered.'

'I will wait for you on the lawn.'

'My head is rather heavy.'

His deep concern and tenderness brought him close.

She assured him sparklingly that she was well: she was ready to accompany him to the garden and stroll over the park.

'Head*ache* it is not,' she said

But she had to pay the fee for inviting a solicitous accepted gentleman's proximity.

This time she blamed herself and him, and the world he abused, and destiny into the bargain. And she cared less about the probation; but she craved for liberty. With a frigidity that astonished her, she marvelled at the act of kissing, and at the obligation it forced upon an inanimate person to be an accomplice. Why was she not free? By what strange right was it that she was treated as a possession?

15 Marriage for the Wrong Reasons —or to the Wrong Man

From *Portrait of a Lady*

by Henry James

Henry James was an American born in 1843 into a famous family of philosophers. In his thirties he settled in Europe and in 1898 went to live in Rye, Sussex. He was awarded the O.M. (after becoming a naturalised Briton) and died in 1916. He is well-known for short stories, novels and criticisms of which the best known are The Turn of the Screw *(a short story),* Washington Square *(popular in its dramatic adaptation),* The Awkward Age, The Wings of the Dove, The Ambassadors, Roderick Hudson, The Europeans *and* The Golden Bowl. *He is famous as a stylist. His long convoluted sentences seem difficult at first but gradually exert a hypnotic effect. His critics say he is too effete, too remote from the preoccupations of ordinary men. He had an interesting correspondence with H. G. Wells (q.v.) on this subject. Two more dissimilar authors could not be found.*

Isabel Archer has married a man whom she believed loved her for herself. She is slowly disillusioned and suffers a great deal.

Isabel's cheek burned when she asked herself if she had really married on a factitious theory, in order to do something finely appreciable with her money. But she was able to answer quickly enough that this was only half the story. It was because a certain ardour took possession of her—a sense of the earnestness of his affection and a delight in his personal qualities. He was better than anyone else. This supreme conviction had filled her life for months, and enough of it still remained to prove to her that she could not have done otherwise. The finest—in the sense of being the subtlest—manly organism she had ever known had become her property, and the recognition of her having but to put out her hands and take it had been originally a sort of act of devotion. She had not been mistaken about the beauty of his mind; she knew that organ perfectly now. She had lived with it, she had lived *in* it almost—it appeared to have become her habitation. If she had been captured it had taken a firm hand to seize her; that reflection perhaps had some worth. A mind more ingenious, more pliant, more cultivated, more trained to admirable exercises, she had not encountered; and it was this exquisite instrument she had now to reckon with. She lost herself in infinite dismay when she thought of the magnitude of *his* deception. It was a wonder, perhaps, in view of this, that he didn't hate her more. She remembered perfectly the first sign he had given of it—it had been like the bell that was to ring up the curtain upon the real drama of their life. He said to her one day that she had too many ideas and that she must get rid of them. He had told her that already, before their marriage; but then she had not noticed it: it had come back to her only afterwards. This time she might well have noticed it, because he had really meant it. The words had been nothing superficially, but when in the light of deepening experience she had looked into them they had then appeared portentous. He had really meant it—he would have liked her to have nothing of her own but her pretty appearance. She had known she had too many ideas; she had more even than he had supposed, many more than she had expressed to him when he had asked her to marry him. Yes, she *had* been hypocritical she had liked him so much. She had too many ideas for herself; but that was just what one married for, to share them with someone else. One couldn't pluck them up by the roots, though of course one might suppress them, be careful not to utter them. It had not been this, however, his objecting to her opinions; this had been nothing. She had no opinions—none that she would not have been eager to sacrifice in the satisfaction of feeling herself loved for it. What he had meant had been the whole thing—her character, the way she felt, the way she judged. This was what she had kept in reserve; this was what he had not known until he had found himself—with the door closed behind, as it were—set down face to face with it. She had a certain way of looking at life which he took as a personal offence. Heaven knew that now at least it was a very humble, accommodating way! The strange thing was that she should not have suspected from the first that his own had been so different. She had thought it so large, so enlightened, so perfectly that of an honest man and a gentleman. Hadn't he assured her that he had no superstitions, no dull limitations, no prejudices that had lost their freshness? Hadn't he all the appearance of a man living in the open air of the world, indifferent to small considerations, caring only for truth and knowledge and believing that two intelligent people ought to look for them together and, whether they found them or not, find at least some happiness in the search? He had told her he loved the conventional; but there was a sense in which this seemed a noble declaration. In that sense, that of the love of harmony and order and decency and of all the stately offices of life, she went with him freely, and his warning had contained nothing ominous. But when, as the months had elapsed, she had followed him farther and he had led her into the mansion of his own habitation, then, *then* she had seen where she really was.

16 Love and Commonsense

From *Letters*

by Jane Austen

See biography of Jane Austen under Emma, *Extract No. 11.*
Fanny Knight, the eldest daughter of Jane Austen's brother, Edward, was the writer's favourite niece.

Letter to Fanny Knight   *Fri. 18 Nov. 1814.*

Chawton Nov: 18—Friday

I feel quite as doubtful as you could be my dearest Fanny as to *when* my letter may be finished, for I can command very little quiet time at present, but yet I must begin, for I know you will be glad to hear as soon as possible, and I really am impatient myself to be writing something on so very interesting a subject, though I have no hope of writing anything to the purpose. I shall do very little more I dare say than say over again, what you have said before. I was certainly a good deal surprised *at first*—as I had no suspicion of any change in your feelings, and I have no scruple in saying that you cannot be in love. My dear Fanny, I am ready to laugh at the idea—and yet it is no laughing matter to have had you so mistaken as to your own feelings—and with all my heart I wish I had cautioned you on that point when first you spoke to me;—but tho' I did not think you then so *much* in love as you thought yourself, I did consider you as being attached in a degree— quite sufficiently for happiness, as I had no doubt it would increase with opportunity.—And from the time of our being in London together, I thought you really very much in love—but you are certainly not at all—there is no concealing it.—What strange creatures we are!—It seems as if your being secure of him (as you say yourself) had made you indifferent.—There was a little disgust I suspect, at the Races—and I do not wonder at it. His expressions there would not do for one who had rather more Acuteness Penetration and Taste, than Love, which was your care. And yet, after all, I *am* surprised that the change in your feelings should be so great.—He is, just what he ever was, only more evidently and uniformly devoted to *you*. This is all the difference—How shall we account for it? My dearest Fanny, I am writing what will not be of the smallest use to you. I am feeling differently every moment and shall not be able to suggest a single thing that can assist your Mind.—I could lament in one sentence and laugh in the next, but as to Opinion or Counsel I am sure none will be extracted worth having from this Letter. I read yours through the very evening I received it—getting away by myself—I could not bear to leave off, when I had once begun. I was full of curiosity and concern. Luckily your Aunt C. dined at the other house, therefore I had not to manoeuvre away from *her*;—and as to anybody else, I do not care.—Poor dear Mr. J.P.!—Oh! Dear Fanny, your mistake has been one that thousands of women fall into. He was the *first* young man who attached himself to you. That was the charm, and most powerful it is.—Among the multitudes however that make the same mistake with yourself, there can be few indeed who have so little reason to regret it;—*his* Character and *his* attachment leave you nothing to be ashamed of.—Upon the whole, what is to be done? You certainly have encouraged him to such a point as to make him feel almost secure of you—you have no inclination for any other person.—His situation in life, family, friends, and above all his character—his uncommonly amiable mind, strict principles, just notions, good habits—*all* that *you* know so well how to value, *All* that really is of the first importance—everything of this nature pleads his cause most strongly.—You have no doubt of his having superior Abilities—he has proved it at the University—he is I dare say such a scholar as your agreeable, idle Brothers would ill bear a comparison with.—Oh! my dear Fanny, the more I write about him, the warmer my feelings become, the more strongly I feel the shining worth of such a young man and the desirableness of your growing in love with him again. I recommend this most thoroughly—There *are* such beings in the World perhaps, one in a thousand, as the Creature you and I would think perfection, where Grace and Spirit are united to Worth, where the Manners are equal to the Heart and Understanding, but such a person may not come in your way, or if he does, he may not be the eldest son of a Man of Fortune, the Brother of your particular friend, and belonging to your own Country—Think of all this Fanny. Mr. J.P.—has advantages which do not often meet in one person. His only fault indeed seems Modesty. If he were less modest, he would be agreeable, speak louder and look impudenter;— and is not it a fine Character of which Modesty is the only defect?—I have no doubt that he will get more lively and more like yourselves as he is more with you;—he will catch your ways if he belongs to you and as to there being any objection from his *Goodness*, from the danger of his becoming even Evangelical, I cannot admit *that*. I am no means convinced that we ought not all to be Evangelicals, and am at least persuaded that they who are so from Reason and Feeling, must be happiest and safest.—Do not be frightened from the connection from your Brothers having most wit.

Wisdom is better than Wit, and in the long run will certainly have the laugh on her side; and don't be frightened by the idea of his acting more strictly up to the precepts of the New Testament than others.—And now, my dear Fanny, having written so much on one side of the question, I shall turn round and entreat you not to commit yourself farther, and not to think of accepting him unless you really do like him. Anything is to be pretended or endured rather than marrying without Affection; and if his deficiencies of Manner etc., etc., strike you more than all his good qualities, if you continue to think strongly of them, give him up at once.—Things are now in such a state, that you must resolve upon one or the other, either allow him to go on as he has done, or whenever you are together behave with a coldness which may convince him that he has been deceiving himself.—I have no doubt of his suffering a good deal for a time, a great deal, when he feels that he must give you up;—but it is no creed of mine, as you must be well aware, that such sort of disappointments kill anybody. —Your sending the Music was an admirable Device, it made everything easy, and I do not know how I could have accounted for the parcel otherwise; for tho' your dear Papa most conscientiously hunted about till he found me alone in the dining-parlour, your Aunt C. had seen that he *had* a parcel to deliver. As it was however, I do not think anything was suspected.—We have heard nothing fresh from Anna. I trust she is very comfortable in her new home. Her letters have been very sensible and satisfactory, with no *parade* of happiness, which I liked them the better for.— I have often known young married women write in a way I did not like in that respect ...

P.S. Your trying to excite your own feelings by a visit to his room amused me excessively.—The Dirty Shaving Rag was exquisite!—such a circumstance ought to be in print. Much too good to be lost.—Remember me particularly to Fanny C.—I thought you would like to hear from me while you were with her.

17 Advising a Daughter on Life

From *Letters*

by Queen Victoria

Queen Victoria (1819–1901) was a voluminous letter-writer and diarist. This letter is taken from a selection of those to her eldest daughter who married the German Crown Prince and became the mother of Kaiser Wilhelm. The Crown Princess was married at 17 in January 1858 and her first baby was born in January 1859 when Queen Victoria herself was only 39. These letters were written in 1859 and 1860.

What you say of the pride of giving life to an immortal soul is very fine, dear, but I own I cannot enter into that; I think much more of our being like a cow or a dog at such moments; when our poor nature becomes so very animal and unecstatic—but for you, dear, if you are sensible and reasonable not in ecstasy nor spending your day with nurses and wet nurses, which is the ruin of many a refined and intellectual young lady, without adding to her real maternal duties, a child will be a great resource. Above all, dear, do remember never to lose the modesty of a young girl towards others (without being prude); though you are married don't become a matron at once to whom everything can be said, and who minds saying nothing herself—I remained particular to a degree (indeed feel so now) and often feel shocked at the confidences of other married ladies. I fear abroad they are very indelicate about these things. Think of me who at that first time, very unreasonable, and perfectly furious as I was to be caught, having to have drawing rooms and levees and made to sit down—and be stared at and take every sort of precaution.

I know that the little being will be a great reward for all your trouble and suffering—but I know you will not forget, dear, your promise not to indulge in 'baby worship', or to neglect your other greater duties in becoming a nurse. You know how manifold your duties are, and as my dear child is a little disorderly in regulating her time, I fear you might lose a great deal of it, if you overdid the passion for the nursery. No lady, and still less a Princess, is fit for her husband or her position, if she does that. I know, dear, that you will feel and guard against this, but I only just wish to remind you and warn you, as with your great passion for little children (which are mere little plants for the first six months) it would be very natural for you to be carried away by your pleasure at having a child.

* * *

Your dear affectionate letter of the 6th reached me today and I thank you and with all my heart for it. It is quite like your own dear self again and it is a pleasure to see how you feel like me even on all those distressing subjects so painful to a woman's feelings and especially to a young child as you are! Poor dear darling! I pitied you so! It is indeed too hard and dreadful what we have to go through and men ought to have an adoration for one, and indeed to do every thing to make up, for what after all they alone are the cause of! I must say it is a bad arrangement, but we must calmly, patiently bear it, and feel that we can't help it and therefore we must forget it, and the more we retain our pure, modest feelings, the easier it is to get over it all afterwards. I am very much like a girl in all these feelings, but since I have had a grown-up daughter, and young married relations I have been obliged to hear and talk of things and details which I hate—but which are unavoidable.

* * *

I have this very moment received your dear letter of the 18th and thank you much for it. I am glad you bear out what I said about our dear correspondence. It is an immense pleasure and comfort to me, for it is dreadful to live so far off and always separated. I really think I shall never let your sisters marry—certainly not to be so constantly away and see so little of their parents—as till now, you have done, contrary to all that I was originally promised and told. I am so glad to see that you so entirely enter into all my feelings as a mother. Yes, dearest, it is an awful moment to have to give one's innocent child up to a man, be he ever so kind and good—and to think of all that she must go through! I can't say what I suffered, what I felt—what struggles I had to go through—(indeed I have not quite got over it yet) and that last night when we took you to your room, and you cried so much, I said to Papa as we came back 'after all, it is like taking a poor lamb to be sacrificed.' You know now—what I meant, dear. I know that God has willed it so and these are the trials which we poor women must go through; no father, no man can feel this! Papa never would enter into it all! As in fact he seldom can in my very violent feelings. It really makes me shudder when I look around at all your sweet, happy, unconscious sisters —and think that I must give them up too—one by one! Our dear Alice, has seen and heard more (of course not what no one can ever know before they marry and before they have had children) than you did, from your marriage—and quite enough to give her a horror rather of marrying.

* * *

Now I must scold you a wee bit for an observation which really seems at variance with your own expressions. You say 'how glad' Ada 'must be' at being again in that most charming situation, which you yourself very frequently told me last year was so wretched. How can anyone, who has not been married above two years and three quarters, (like Ada) rejoice at being a third time in that condition? I positively think those ladies who are always enceinte quite disgusting; it is more like a rabbit or guinea-pig than anything else and really it is not very nice. There is Lady Kildare who has two a year one in January and one in December—and always is so, whenever one sees her! I know Papa is shocked at that sort of thing. To be truly thankful for the blessing, when one has a child and to be glad to have them leisurely (without which I can assure you, life is wretched

I know this from the experience of the first four years of my marriage) and one becomes so worn out and one's nerves so miserable—I can understand—(though I did not when I was younger). Let me repeat once more, dear, that it is very bad for any person to have them very fast—and that poor children suffer for it, even more, not to speak of the ruin it is to the looks of a young woman—which she must not neglect for her husband's sake, particularly when she is a Princess and obliged to appear.

* * *

... all marriage is such a lottery—the happiness is always an exchange—though it may be a very happy one—still the poor woman is bodily and morally the husband's slave. That always sticks in my throat. When I think of a merry, happy, free young girl—and look at the ailing, aching state a young wife generally is doomed to—which you can't deny is the penalty of marriage.

* * *

18 Being Married

From *At the Bay*

by Katherine Mansfield

Katherine Mansfield was born Kathleen Beauchamp in 1888 in New Zealand. She was educated in England at Queens College, Harley Street and finally returned to England for good in 1908. She had written stories and poems from an early age. She met and later married John Middleton Murry and was also a great friend of D. H. Lawrence.

She died of tuberculosis in France in 1923. Her publications include In a German Pension, 1911, Bliss, 1920, The Garden Party, 1922, Journal, *(published posthumously in 1927) and* Letters *(1929 and 1951 posthumously). This extract comes from one of the stories in* The Garden Party. *There is an excellent life of Katherine Mansfield by Antony Alpers. She is one of those writers who are almost better known as literary figures than as authors of actual books. She has had great influence and is one of the best writers of short stories in English.*

'Wait a minute—have you children been playing with my stick?'

'No, father!'

'But I put it here,' Stanley began to bluster. 'I remember distinctly putting it in this corner. Now, who's had it? There's no time to lose. Look sharp! The stick's got to be found.'

Even Alice, the servant girl, was drawn into the chase. 'You haven't been using it to poke the kitchen fire with by any chance?'

Stanley dashed into the bedroom where Linda was lying. 'Most extraordinary thing. I can't keep a single possession to myself. They've made away with my stick, now!'

'Stick, dear? What stick?' Linda's vagueness on these occasions could not be real, Stanley decided. Would nobody sympathise with him?

'Coach! Coach, Stanley!' Beryl's voice from the gate.

Stanley waved his arm to Linda. 'No time to say good-bye!' he cried. And he meant that as a punishment to her.

He snatched his bowler hat, dashed out of the house, and swung down the garden path. Yes, the coach was there waiting, and Beryl, leaning over the open gate, was laughing up at somebody or other just as if nothing had happened. The heartlessness of women! The way they took it for granted it was your job to slave away for them while they didn't even take the trouble to see that your walking-stick wasn't lost. Kelly trailed his whip across the horses.

'Good-bye, Stanley,' called Beryl, sweetly and gaily. It was easy enough to say good-bye! And there she stood, idle, shading her eyes with her hand. The worst of it was Stanley had to shout good-bye too, for the sake of appearances. Then he saw her turn, give a little skip and run back to the house. She was glad to be rid of him!

Yes, she was thankful. Into the living-room she ran and called 'He's gone!' Linda cried from her room: 'Beryl! Has Stanley gone?' Old Mrs. Fairfield appeared, carrying the boy in his little flannel coatee.

'Gone?'

'Gone!'

Oh, the relief, the difference it made to have the man out of the house. Their very voices were changed as they called to one another; they sounded warm and loving and as if they shared a secret. Beryl went over to the table. 'Have another cup of tea, mother. It's still hot.' She wanted, somehow, to celebrate the fact that they could do what they liked now. There was no man to disturb them; the whole perfect day was theirs.

'No, thank you, child,' said old Mrs. Fairfield, but the way at that moment she tossed the boy up and said 'a-goos-a-goos-a-ga!' to him meant that she felt the same. The little girls ran into the paddock like chickens let out of a coop.

Even Alice, the servant girl, washing up the dishes in

the kitchen, caught the infection and used the precious tank water in a perfectly reckless fashion.

'Oh, these men!' said she, and she plunged the teapot into the bowl and held it under the water even after it had stopped bubbling, as if it too was a man and drowning was too good for them.

* * *

Linda frowned; she sat up quickly in her steamer chair and clasped her ankles. Yes, that was her real grudge against life; that was what she could not understand. That was the question she asked and asked, and listened in vain for the answer. It was all very well to say it was the common lot of women to bear children. It wasn't true. She, for one, could prove that wrong. She was broken, made weak, her courage was gone, through child-bearing. And what made it doubly hard to bear was, she did not love her children. It was useless pretending. Even if she had had the strength she never would have nursed and played with the little girls. No, it was as though a cold breath had chilled her through and through on each of those awful journeys; she had no warmth left to give them. As to the boy—well, thank heaven, mother had taken him; he was mother's, or Beryl's, or anybody's who wanted him. She had hardly held him in her arms. She was so indifferent about him, that as he lay there ... Linda glanced down.

The boy had turned over. He lay facing her, and he was no longer asleep. His dark-blue, baby eyes were open; he looked as though he was peeping at his mother. And suddenly his face dimpled; it broke into a wide, toothless smile, a perfect beam, no less.

'I'm here!' that happy smile seemed to say. 'Why don't you like me?'

There was something so quaint, so unexpected about that smile that Linda smiled herself. But she checked herself and said to the boy coldly, 'I don't like babies.'

'Don't like babies?' the boy couldn't believe her. 'Don't like *me*?' He waved his arms foolishly at his mother.

Linda dropped off her chair on to the grass. 'Why do you keep on smiling?' she said severely. 'If you knew what I was thinking about, you wouldn't.' But he only squeezed up his eyes, slyly, and rolled his head on the pillow. He didn't believe a word she said. 'We know all about that!' smiled the boy. Linda was so astonished at the confidence of this little creature . . . Ah, no, be sincere. That was not what she felt; it was something far different, it was something so new, so . . . The tears danced in her eyes; she breathed in a small whisper to the boy, 'Hello my funny!'

But by now the boy had forgotten his mother. He was serious again. Something pink, something soft waved in front of him. He made a grab at it and it immediately disappeared. But when he lay back, another, like the first, appeared. This time he determined to catch it. He made a tremendous effort and rolled right over.

19 Being Married—and a Little Older

From *To The Lighthouse*

by Virginia Woolf

See biography of Virginia Woolf under The Waves, *Extract No. 2.*
Mrs. Ramsay, the 'heroine' of this novel is a person who has made an art of living, extending each perfect moment into something permanent and giving people who know her the impression that somehow everything is simple although the meaning of life still eludes them. In fact for almost half the novel Mrs. Ramsay has died. We see her very much through the eyes of an artist, Lily Briscoe. We know that she was and is beautiful, has had eight children and adores her husband but she is something of a mystery and it is her effect on others which seems to stand as a symbol of a rounded and complete woman. To herself '... So boasting of her capacity to surround and protect, there was scarcely a shell of herself left for her to know herself by; all was so lavished and spent....'

No, she thought, putting together some of the pictures he had cut out—a refrigerator, a mowing machine, a gentleman in evening dress—children never forget. For this reason it was so important what one said, and what one did, and it was a relief when they went to bed. For now she need not think about anybody. She could be herself, by herself. And that was what now she often felt the need of—to think; well not even to think. To be silent; to be alone. All the being and the doing, expansive, glittering, vocal, evaporated; and one shrunk, with a sense of solemnity, to being oneself, a wedge-shaped core of darkness, something invisible to others. Although she continued to knit, and sat upright, it was thus that she felt herself; and this self having shed its attachments was free for the strangest adventures. When life sank down for a moment, the range of experience seemed limitless. And to everybody there was always this sense of unlimited resources, she supposed; one after another, she, Lily, Augustus Carmichael, must feel, our apparitions, the things you know us by, are simply childish. Beneath it is all dark, it is all spreading, it is unfathomably deep; but now and again we rise to the surface and that is what you see us by. Her horizon seemed to her limitless. There were all the places she had not seen; the Indian plains; she felt herself pushing aside the thick leather curtain of a church in Rome. This core of darkness could go anywhere, for no one saw it. They could not stop it, she thought, exulting. There was freedom, there was peace, there was, most welcome of all, a summoning together, a resting on a platform of stability. Not as oneself did one find rest ever, in her experience (she accomplished here something dexterous with her needles), but as a wedge of darkness. Losing personality, one lost the fret, the hurry, the stir; and there rose to her lips always some exclamation of triumph over life when things came together in this peace, this rest, this eternity; and pausing there she looked out to meet that stroke of the Lighthouse, the long steady stroke, the last of the three, which was her stroke, for watching them in this mood always at this hour one could not help attaching oneself to one thing especially of the things one saw; and this thing, the long steady stroke, was her stroke. Often she found herself sitting and looking, sitting and looking, with her work in her hands until she became the thing she looked at—that light for example. And it would lift up on it some little phrase or other which had been lying in her mind like that—'Children don't forget, children don't forget'—which she would repeat and begin adding to it, It will end, It will end, she said. It will come, it will come, when suddenly she added: We are in the hands of the Lord.

But instantly she was annoyed with herself for saying that. Who had said it? not she; she had been trapped into saying something she did not mean. She looked up over her knitting and met the third stroke and it seemed to her like her own eyes meeting her own eyes, searching as she alone could search into her mind and her heart, purifying out of existence that lie, any lie. She praised herself in praising the light, without vanity, for she was stern, she was searching, she was beautiful like that light. It was odd, she thought, how if one was alone, one leant to things, inanimate things; trees, streams, flowers; felt they expressed one; felt they became one; felt they knew one, in a sense were one; felt an irrational tenderness thus (she looked at that long steady light) as for oneself. There rose, and she looked and looked with her needles suspended, there curled up off the floor of the mind, rose from the lake of one's being, a mist, a bride to meet her lover.

What brought her to say that: 'We are in the hands of the Lord?' she wondered. The insincerity slipping in among the truths roused her, annoyed her. She returned to her knitting again. How could any Lord have made this world? she asked. With her mind she had always seized the fact that there is no reason, order, justice: but suffering, death, the poor. There was no treachery too base for the world to commit; she knew that. No happiness lasted; she knew that. She knitted with firm composure, slightly pursing her lips and, without being aware of it, so stiffened and composed the lines of her face in a habit of sternness that when her husband passed, though he was chuckling at the thought that Hume, the philosopher, grown enormously fat, had stuck in a bog, he could not help noting, as he passed, the sternness at the heart of her beauty. It saddened him, and her remoteness pained him, and he felt, as he passed, that he could not protect her, and, when he reached the hedge, he was sad. He could do nothing to help her. He must stand by and watch her. Indeed, the infernal truth was, he made things worse for her. He was irritable—he was touchy. He had lost his temper over the Lighthouse. He looked into the hedge, into its intricacy, its darkness.

Always, Mrs. Ramsay felt, one helped oneself out of solitude reluctantly by laying hold of some little odd or end, some sound, some sight. She listened, but it was all very still; cricket was over; the children were in their baths;

there was only the sound of the sea. She stopped knitting; she held the long reddish-brown stocking dangling in her hands a moment. She saw the light again. With some irony in her interrogation, for when one woke at all, one's relations changed, she looked at the steady light, the pitiless, the remorseless, which was so much her, yet so little her, which had her at its beck and call (she woke in the night and saw it bent across their bed, stroking the floor), but for all that she thought, watching it with fascination, hypnotized, as if it were stroking with its silver fingers some sealed vessel in her brain whose bursting would flood her with delight, she had known happiness, exquisite happiness, intense happiness, and it silvered the rough waves a little more brightly, as daylight faded, and the blue went out of the sea and it rolled in waves of pure lemon which curved and swelled and broke upon the beach and the ecstasy burst in her eyes and waves of pure delight raced over the floor of her mind and she felt, It is enough! It is enough!

He turned and saw her. Ah! She was lovely, lovelier now than ever he thought. But he could not speak to her. He could not interrupt her. He wanted urgently to speak to her now that James was gone and she was alone at last. But he resolved, no; he would not interrupt her. She was aloof from him now in her beauty, in her sadness. He would let her be, and he passed her without a word, though it hurt him that she should look so distant, and he could not reach her, he could do nothing to help her. And again he would have passed her without a word had she not, at that very moment, given him of her own free will what she knew he would never ask, and called to him and taken the green shawl off the picture frame, and gone to him. For he wished, she knew, to protect her.

20 Being a Bluestocking Married to a Genius

From *Letters*

by Jane Welsh Carlyle

Jane Welsh Carlyle (1801–1866) was the Scottish wife of the sage Thomas Carlyle and is chiefly known through her letters which she wrote in enormous numbers. She lived in Cheyne Walk, Chelsea and wrote copiously to her husband whenever they were apart.

To Miss Mary Smith,*   5, Cheyne Row,
Carlisle.   Chelsea.
       January 11th, 1857.

Dear Miss Smith,

This time you come to me as an old acquaintance whom I am glad to shake hands with again. The mere fact of your being still in the same position after so long an interval, and with such passionate inward protest as that first letter indicated, is a more authentic testimony of your worth, than if you had sent me a certificate of character signed by all the clergy and householders of Carlisle! So many talents are wasted, so many enthusiasms turned to smoke, so many lived blighted for want of a little patience and endurance, for want of understanding and laying to heart that which you have so well expressed in these verses—the meaning of *the Present*—for want of recognising that it is not the greatness or littleness of 'the duty nearest hand', but the spirit in which one does it, that makes one's doing noble or mean!

I can't think how people who have any natural ambition,

---

* Miss Mary Smith was a governess and teacher in Carlisle who wanted to be a writer. She had written to Mrs. Carlyle some years before to ask for her help.

and any sense of power in them, escape going *mad* in a world like this, without the recognition of that! I know I was very near mad when I found it out for myself (as one has to find out for oneself everything that is to be of any real practical use to one). Shall I tell you how it came into my head? Perhaps it may be of comfort to you in similar moments of fatigue and disgust.

I had gone with my husband to live on a little estate of *peat bog* that had descended to me, all the way down from John Welsh, the Covenanter, who married a daughter of John Knox. *That* didn't, I'm ashamed to say, make me feel Craigenputtock a whit less of a peat bog, and most dreary, untoward place to live at. In fact, it was sixteen miles distance on every side from all the conveniences of life —shops, and even post office!

Further, we were very *poor* and, further and worst, being an only child, and brought up to 'great prospects', I was sublimely ignorant of every branch of useful knowledge, though a capital Latin scholar and a very fair mathematician!! It behoved me in these shocking circumstances to learn—to sew! Husbands, I was shocked to find, wore their stockings into holes! And were always losing buttons! and I was expected to 'look to all that'. Also, it behoved me to learn to *cook*! No capable servant choosing to live at 'such an out of the way place', and my husband having 'bad digestion' which complicated my difficulties dreadfully. The *bread* above all, brought from Dumfries, 'soured on his stomach' (oh Heavens!); and it was plainly my duty as a Christian wife to bake at home! So I sent for Cobbett's *Cottage Economy* and fell to work at a loaf of bread. But knowing nothing of the process of fermentation or the heat of ovens, it came to pass that my loaf got put into the oven at the time myself ought to have been put into bed, and I remained the only person not asleep, in a house in the middle of a desert! One o'clock struck, and then two and then three; and still I was sitting there in an intense solitude, my whole body aching with weariness, my heart aching with a sense of forlornness and *degradation*. 'That I who had been so petted at home, whose comfort had been studied by everybody in the house, who had never been required to *do* anything but *cultivate my mind* should have to pass all those hours of the night watching *a loaf of bread*! which mightn't turn out bread after all!'

Such thoughts maddened me, till I laid my head on the table and sobbed aloud. It was then that somehow the idea of Benvenuto Cellini's sitting up all night watching his Perseus* in the oven, came into my head; and suddenly I asked myself, 'After all, in the sight of the upper powers, what is the mighty difference between a statue of Perseus and a loaf of bread, so that each be the thing one's hand hath found to do? The man's determined will, his energy, his patience, his resource, were the really admirable things of which the state of Perseus, was the mere chance expression. If he had been a woman living at Craigenputtock, with a dyspeptic husband, sixteen miles from a baker, *and he a bad one*, all these same qualities would have come out most fitting in a *good* loaf of bread!'

I cannot express what consolation this germ of an idea spread over an uncongenial life, during five years we lived at that savage place; where my two immediate predecessors had gone *mad*, and the third had taken to *drink*.

* This word is Pericles in Miss Smith's Autobiography, but it is undoubtedly a copyist's error; Mrs. Carlyle would never have written anything but Perseus . . . T.B. ed. 'Jane Welsh Carlyle'.

21 Wanting a Life of One's Own

From *All Passion Spent*

by Victoria Sackville-West

Victoria Sackville-West was born in 1892 and died in 1962. She wrote poetry and novels of which the best-known are All Passion Spent, *1931, and* The Easter Party, *1953. Her long poem 'The Land' was perhaps her best. She was also a biographer and a great friend of Virginia Woolf (who took her as model for the enigmatic 'Orlando'). Her gardens at Sissinghurst are famous throughout England.*

Indeed, these weeks before the wedding were dedicated wholly to the rites of a mysterious feminism. Never, Deborah thought, had she been surrounded by so many women. Matriarchy ruled. Men might have dwindled into insignificance on the planet. Even Henry himself did not count for much. (Yet he was there, terribly there, in the background; and thus, she thought, might a Theban mother have tired her daughter before sending her off to the Minotaur). Women appeared from all quarters: aunts, cousins, friends, dressmakers, corsetieres, milliners, and even a young French maid, whom Deborah was to have for her own, and who regarded her new mistress with wondering eyes, as one upon whom the gods had set their seal. In these rites Deborah—another assumption—was expected to play a most complicated part. She was expected to know what it was all about, and yet the core of the mystery was to remain hidden from her. She was to be the recipient of smiling congratulations, yet also she must be addressed as 'My little Deborah!' an exclamation from which she suspected that the adjective 'poor' was missing just by chance, and clipped in long embraces, almost valedictory in their benevolence. Oh, what a pother, she thought, women make about marriage! and yet who can blame them, she added, when one recollects that marriage—and its consequence—is the only thing that women have to make a pother about in the whole of their lives? Though the excitement be vicarious, it will do just as well. Is it not for this function that they have been formed, dressed, bedizened, educated—if so one-sided an affair may be called education—safeguarded, kept in the dark, hinted at, segregated, repressed, all that at a given moment they may be delivered, or may deliver their daughters over, to Minister to a Man?

But how on earth she was going to minister to him, Deborah did not know. She knew only that she remained alien to all this fuss about the wonderful opportunity which was to be hers. She supposed that she was not in love with Henry, but, even had she been in love with him, she could see therein no reason for foregoing the whole of her separate existence. Henry was in love with her, but no one proposed that he should forego his. On the contrary, it appeared that in acquiring her he was merely adding something extra to it. He would continue to lunch with his friends, travel down to his constituency and spend his evenings at the House of Commons; he would continue to enjoy his free, varied, and masculine life, with no ring upon his finger or difference in his name to indicate the change in his estate; but whenever he felt inclined to come home she must be there, ready to lay down her book, her paper, or her letters; she must be prepared to listen to whatever he had to say; she must entertain his political acquaintances, and even if he beckoned her across the world she must follow. Well, she thought, that recalled Ruth and Boaz and was very pleasant for Henry. No doubt he would do his part by her, as he understood it. Sitting down by her, as her needle plocked in and out of her embroidery, he would gaze fondly at her bent head, and would say he was lucky to have such a pretty little wife to come back to. For all his grandeur as a Cabinet Minister, he would say it like any middle-class or working-man husband. And she ought to look up, rewarded. For all his grandeur and desirability as Governor or Viceroy, he would disregard the blandishments of women ambitious for their husbands, beyond the necessary gallantries of social intercourse, and would be faithful to her, so that the green snake of jealousy would never slip across her path. He would advance in honours, and with a genuine pride would see a coronet appear on the head of the little black shadow which had doubled him for so many years. But where, in such a programme, was there room for a studio?

It would not do if Henry were to return one evening and be met by a locked door. It would not do if Henry, short of ink or blotting paper, were to emerge irritably only to be told that Mrs. Holland were engaged with a model. It would not do if Henry were appointed governor to some distant colony, to tell him that the drawing master unfortunately lived in London. It would not do if Henry wanted another son, to tell him that she had just embarked on a special course of study. It would not do in such a world of assumptions, to assume that she had equal rights with Henry. For such privileges marriage was not ordained.

But for certain privileges marriage had been ordained, and going to her bedroom Deborah took out her prayerbook and turned up the Marriage Service. It was ordained for the procreation of children—well she knew that; one of her friends had told her, before she had time to stop her ears. It was ordained so that women might be loving and amiable, faithful and obedient to their husbands, holy and godly matrons in all quietness, sobriety and peace. All this no doubt was, to a certain extent, parliamentary language. But still it bore a certain relation to fact. And still she asked where, in this system, was there room for a studio?

Henry, always charming and courteous, and now very much in love, smiled most indulgently when she finally brought herself to ask him if he would object to her painting after they were married. Object! Of course he would not object. He thought an elegant accomplishment most becoming in a woman. 'I confess,' he said, 'that of all feminine accomplishments the piano is my favourite, but since your talent lies in another direction, my dearest, why then we'll make the best of it: And he went on to say how pleasant it would be for them both if she kept a record of their travels, and mentioned something about water-colour sketches in an album, which they could show their friends at home. But when Deborah said that that was not quite what she had in mind—she had thought something more serious, she said, though her heart was in her mouth as she said it—he had smiled again, more fondly and indulgently than ever, and has said there would be plenty of time to see about that, but for his own part, he fancied that after marriage she would find plenty of other occupations to help her pass the days.

Then, indeed, she felt trapped and wild. She knew very well what he meant. She hated him for his Jovian detachment and superiority, for his fond but nevertheless smug assumptions, for his easy kindliness, and most of all for the impossibility of blaming him. He was not to blame. He had only taken for granted the things he was entitled to take for granted, thereby ranging himself with the women and entering into the general conspiracy to defraud her of her chosen life.

She was very childish, very tentative, very uncertain, very unaware. But at least she did recognise that the conversation had been momentous. She had her answer. She never referred to it again.

Yet she was no feminist. She was too wise a woman, to indulge in such luxuries as an imagined martyrdom. The rift between herself and life was not the rift between man and woman, but the rift between the worker and the dreamer. That she was a woman, and Henry a man, was really a matter of chance. She would go no further than to acknowledge that the fact of her being a woman made the situation a degree more difficult....

She was, after all, a woman. Thwarted as an artist, was it perhaps possible to find fulfilment in other ways? Was there, after all, some foundation for the prevalent belief that women should minister to man? Had the generations been right, the personal struggle wrong? Was there something beautiful, something active, something creative even, in her apparent submission to Henry? Could she not balance herself upon the tight-rope of her relationship with him, as dangerously and precariously as in the act of creating a picture? Was it not possible to see the tones and half-tones of her life with him as she might have seen the blue and violet shadows of a landscape; and so set them in relation and ordain their values, that she thereby toned them into beauty? Was not this also an achievement of the sort peculiarly suited to women? Of the sort, indeed, which women alone could compass; a privilege, a prerogative, not to be despised? All the woman in her answered, yes! All the artist in her countered, no!

And then again, were not women in their new Protestant spirit defrauding the world of some poor remnant of enchantment, some illusion, foolish perhaps, but lovely? This time the woman and the artist in her alike answered, yes.

22 Escaping Temporarily

From *A View of the Harbour*

by Elizabeth Taylor

*Elizabeth Taylor was born in 1912 and had her first novel published just after the war (*At Mrs. Lippincote's*). Others are* Palladian, *1947,* A View of the Harbour, *1949,* A Wreath of Roses, *1950,* A Game of Hide and Seek, *1951,* The Sleeping Beauty, *1953,* Angel, *1957,* In a Summer Season, *1961, and* The Soul of Kindness, *1964. She has also written many short stories, collected variously. She writes with great humour and a sure story teller's touch and some of her best work is about children, young girls, love affairs and the domestic and inner life of women.*

It did rain. In the end Beth went to London in her Burberry and an old felt hat. She carried her night things in a battered hat-box, and took with her some string bags. She did not look at all like Tory's idea of what reviewers sometimes call 'lady novelists', but more like some sensible shopping woman. She also took a new exercise-book, hoping to bring Allegra to her last haven during the train journey. She yearned for the peace and quiet of the railway compartment, as Proust probably yearned for his padded, sound-proof study.

'You will miss that train!' Robert called up the stairs.

'I am just coming, dear.'

It had seemed at that moment as if the sky had suddenly lightened, as if it were going to be a fine, hot day after all, and she was wearing all the wrong clothes; too late to change. She dashed some white powder round her nose and in the middle of her forehead.

'The stew is in the casserole for tonight, Prue,' she called.

'You've told me three times.'

'Don't be rude to your mother,' Robert said sharply.

'This is for you to wear,' Stevie said, holding out a large enamelled butterfly which Beth pinned hastily to her suit.

'It won't show inside your rainingtosh.'

'But when the sun comes out I shall take it off and show everyone the glory.' Beth began to go down the stairs. 'Here I am, Robert. I left the note about the baker on the kitchen dresser. Please ask Mrs. Flitcroft to iron Stevie's frock for tomorrow.'

'Beth, you will *have* to come,' Robert said very quietly, very distinctly.

'That drawing of Steveie's foot for the new shoes!'

'Where did you put it?'

'Behind the clock.'

Now they were all flying about and shouting: the cats went distracted.

'Here it is!' Robert cried. 'We are now going, Beth.'

Outside the front door Beth stooped to kiss Stevie.

'I don't want you to go,' she wailed, twining her arms tightly round her mother's neck, pushing her hat over her eyes.

'Don't be silly, dear. Have a nice day with Edward and Tory.'

'I don't want to be left.'

'Stevie, go indoors,' Robert commanded.

'I want to go to London.'

Her mouth slowly opened, her face crimsoned, then the tears fell, fluently, easily. 'I haven't *ever* been to London.'

'You went to see *Peter Pan*, darling.'

'I didn't like it. I didn't enjoy that day.'

'Beth, don't argue with her.'

'But, sweetest, you know how you loved it at the time, and if you are a good girl I will take you to see it again another day.'

'I saw the wires. I saw the wires,' Stevie screamed, becoming slightly hysterical. 'When they flew, I saw the wires.'

'If we are going to stand here in the road discussing *Peter Pan*, I'll say good-bye,' Robert began.

'I can't leave her like this,' Beth said over her shoulder.

'I missed all that on the ship when I had to go out and be excused,' Stevie bawled. 'I missed the best part.'

Robert began slowly to walk away.

'You are always going and leaving me,' Stevie said; and Beth felt the injustice of this so keenly that she could not go without defending herself.

Tory's door opened and she came flying out, wearing the lilac overall in which she so neatly did her housework.

'Darling Beth, please go. She is just enjoying a little scene and she must not be indulged. As soon as you have gone she will lose interest in it.' She led Stevie into her own house.

'She wants a damned good thrashing,' said Robert, that mild man.

Beth's forehead had begun to pulse. 'I don't want to go,' she said unhappily.

'Don't *you* start,' Robert said, holding open the car door.

At the station, having bought Beth's ticket for her, Robert said good-bye and told her to have a nice time, endeavouring not to know that her heart was torn in two.

'Go to the theatre!' he added robustly, handing over the hat-box. 'Enjoy yourself! None of this moping about round the Elgin Marbles that seems to be your idea of a good time. Snap out of yourself a bit.'

Beth looked at him in amazement. He sounded quite unhinged, she thought. As he never kissed her in public, they merely smiled vaguely and drifted apart; she towards her waiting train and he out into the rainy station yard.

She sat down in the carriage and closed her eyes. Her forehead hammered dully. 'Prudence. Stevie. Robert. Had Stevie stopped screaming yet?' she wondered. 'I am a bad mother,' she once more told herself and fought back the feelings of shame and oppression which assailed her at this admission. 'When I have finished this book I will never write another word. I'll devote myself to Stevie, get Prue married somehow, turn Robert's shirt-cuffs, have the hall repapered. I'll get a proper maid; (for the end of authorship would begin the season of miracles, she felt), 'early morning tea to please Robert, constant hot water, new loose covers. And I will have a freshly-laundered overall twice a week, like Tory, and flowers in all the rooms. Then, perhaps, when we are all reorganized I shall be able to write a short story here and there. None of that drugged sinking into a different world. No more guilt.'

She sat with her eyes closed and the train seemed to stretch itself and gather its great length forward out of the fish-smelling station to the open sky along the shoulders of cliffs.

'A man,' she thought suddenly, 'would consider this a business outing. But, then, a man would not have to cook the meals for the day overnight, nor consign his child to a friend, nor leave half done the ironing, nor forget the grocery order as I now discover I have forgotten it. The artfulness of men,' she thought. 'They implant in us, foster in us, instincts which it is to their advantage for us to have, and which, in the end, we feel shame at not possessing.' She opened her eyes and glared with scorn at a middle-aged man reading a newspaper.

'A man like *that*,' she thought, 'a worthless creature, obviously; yet so long has his kind lorded it that I (who, if only I could have been ruthless and single-minded about my work as men are, could have been a good writer) feel slightly guilty at not being back at the kitchen sink.'

The man began to shift uneasily under her scrutiny, to fold his arms and clear his throat and glance out of the window; so Beth, coming again to her senses, took out her writing things and wrote Chapter Eighteen at the head of a page. But she could not go on. Her spirits were too low to describe Allegra's death. She had looked forward to it so much, but now as she watched fields flying by, wondering where to begin, it was not Allegra's face which interposed, but Stevie's, crimson and tear-furrowed.

23 How Life Passes

From *Tenterhooks*

by Ada Leverson

*Ada Leverson was born in 1862 and died in 1933. Her six novels, originally published between 1907 and 1916 were reissued in 1951. The themes of her 'comedies' are love and friendship. She was an extremely witty writer yet there is an undertone of ironic tragedy. To the literary world she was known as 'The Sphinx'. The three books about Edith Ottley—*Love's Shadow, Tenterhooks *and* Love at Second Sight *are generally agreed to be her best. The public at large knew her best for her loyal friendship with Oscar Wilde.*

Edith was expecting Aylmer to call that afternoon before he went away. She was surprised to find how perturbed she was at the idea of his going away. He had become almost a part of their daily existence, and seeing him was certainly quite the most amusing and exciting experience she had ever had. And now it was coming to an end. Some obscure clairvoyance told her that his leaving and telling her of it in this vague way had some reference to her; but perhaps (she thought) she was wrong; perhaps it was simply that, after the pleasant intercourse and semi-intimacy of the last few weeks, he was going to something that interested him more? He was a widower; and still a young man. Perhaps he was in love with someone. This idea was far from agreeable, although except the first and second time they met he had never said a word that could be described even as flirtation. He showed admiration for her, and pleasure in her society, but he rarely saw her alone. The few visits and tête-à-têtes had always begun by conventional commonplace phrases and embarrassment, and had ended in a delightful sympathy, in animated conversation, in a flowing confidence and gaiety, and in long discussions on books, and art, and principally people. That was all. In fact he had become, in two or three weeks, in a sense *l'ami de la maison*; they went everywhere with him and met nearly every day, and Bruce appeared to adore him. It was entirely different from her long and really intimate friendship with Vincy. Vincy was her confidant, her friend. She could tell him everything, and she did, and he confided in her and told her all except one side of his life, of which she was aware, but to which she never referred. This was his secret romance with a certain girl artist of whom he never spoke, although Edith knew that some day he would tell her about that also.

But with Aylmer there was, and would always be, less real freedom and impersonal frankness, because there was so much more selfconsciousness; in fact because there was an unacknowledged but very strong mutual physical attraction. Edith had, however, felt until now merely the agreeable excitement of knowing that a man she liked, and in whom she was immensely interested, was growing apparently devoted to her, while she had always believed that she would know how to deal with the case in such a way that it could never lead to anything more—that is to say, to more than she wished.

And now, he was going away. Why? And where? However, the first thing to consider was that she would see him today. The result of this consideration was the obvious one. She must do some shopping.

Edith was remarkably feminine in every attribute, in manner, in movement and in appearance; indeed, for a woman of the present day unusually and refreshingly feminine. Yet she had certain mental characteristics which were entirely unlike most women. One was her extreme aversion for shops, and indeed for going into any concrete little details. It has been said that her feeling for dress was sure and unerring. But it was entirely that of the artist; it was impressionistic. Edith was very clever, indeed, most ingenious, in managing practical affairs, as long as she was the director, the general of the campaign. But she did not like carrying out in detail her plans. She liked to be the architect, not the workman.

For example, the small household affairs in the flat went on wheels; everything was almost always perfect. But Edith did not rattle her housekeeping keys, or count the coals, nor did she even go through accounts, or into the kitchen every day. The secret was simple. She had a good cook and housekeeper, who managed all these important but tedious details admirably, under her suggestions. In order to do this Edith had to practise a little fraud on Bruce, a justifiable and quite unselfish one. She gave the cook and housekeeper a quarter of her dress allowance, in addition to the wages Bruce considered sufficient; because Bruce believed that they could not afford more than a certain amount for a cook, while he admitted that Edith, who had a few hundred pounds a year of her own, might need to spend this on dress. Very little of it went on dress, although Edith was not very economical. But she had a plan of her own; she knew that to be dressed in a very ordinary style (that is to say, simple, conventional, *comme il faut*) suited her, by throwing her unusual beauty into relief. Occasionally a touch of individuality was added, when she wanted to have a special effect. But she never entered a shop; very rarely interviewed a milliner. It was always done for her. She was easy to dress, being tall, slim and remarkably pretty. She thought that most women make a great mistake in allowing dress to be the master instead of the servant of their good looks; many women were, she considered, entirely crushed and made insignificant by the beauty of their clothes. The important thing was to have a distinguished appearance, and this cannot, of course, easily be obtained without expensive elegance. But Edith was twenty-eight, and looked younger, so she could dress simply.

This morning Edith had telephoned to her friend, Miss Bennett, an old school-fellow who had nothing to do, and adored commissions. Edith sitting by the fire or at the 'phone, gave her orders, which were always decisive, short and yet meticulous. Miss Bennett was a little late this morning, and Edith had been getting quite anxious to see her. When she at last arrived—she was a nondescript-looking girl, with a small hat squashed on her head, a serge coat and skirt, black gloves and shoes with spats—Edith greeted her rather reproachfully with:

'You're late, Grace.'

'Sorry,' said Grace.

The name suited her singularly badly. She was plain, but had a pleasant face, a pink complexion, small bright eyes, protruding teeth and a scenario for a figure, merely a collection of bones on which a dress could be hung. She was devoted to Edith, and to a few other friends of both sexes, of whom she made idols. She was hard, abrupt, enthusiastic, ignorant and humorous.

'Sorry, but I had to do a lot of—'

'All right,' interrupted Edith. 'You couldn't help it. Listen to what I want you to do.'

'Go ahead,' said Miss Bennett, taking out a note-book and pencil.

Edith spoke in her low, soft, impressive voice, rather slowly.

'Go anywhere you like and bring me back two or three perfectly simple tea-gowns—you know the sort of shape, rather like evening cloaks—straight lines—none of the new draperies and curves—in red, blue and black.'

'On appro.?' asked Miss Bennett.

'On anything you like but made of Liberty satin, with a dull surface.'

'There's no such thing.' Grace Bennett laughed. 'You mean charmeuse, or crepe-de-chine, perhaps?'

'Call it what you like, only get it. You must bring them back in a taxi.'

'Extravagant girl!'

'They're not to cost more than—oh! not much,' added Edith, 'at the most.'

'Economical woman! Why not have a really good tea gown while you're about it?'

'These will be good. I want to have a hard outline like a Fergusson.'

'Oh, really? What's that?'

'Never mind. And suppose you can't get the shape, Grace.'

'Yes?'

'Bring some evening cloaks—the kimonoish kind—I could wear one over a lace blouse; it would look exactly the same.'

'Edith, what curious ideas you have! But you're right enough. Anything else?' said Miss Bennett, standing up, ready to go. 'I like shopping for you. You know what you want.'

'Buy me an azalea, not a large one, and a bit of some dull material of the same colour to drape round it.'

'How extraordinary it is the way you hate anything shiny!' exclaimed Miss Bennett, making a note.

'I know; I only like *matt* effects. Oh, and in case I choose a light-coloured gown, get me just one very large black velvet orchid, too.'

'Right. That all?'

Edith looked at her shoes; they were perfect, tiny, pointed and made of black suede. She decided they would do.

'Yes, that's all, dear.'

'And might I kindly ask,' said Miss Bennett, getting up, 'any particular reason for all this? Are you going to have the flu, or a party, or what?'

'No,' said Edith, who was always frank when it was possible. 'I'm expecting a visitor who's never seen me in anything but a coat and skirt, or in evening dress.'

'Oh! He wants a change, does he?'

'Don't be vulgar, Grace. Thanks awfully, dear. You're really kind.'

They both laughed, and Edith gently pushed her friend out of the room. Then she sat down on a sofa, put up her feet, and began to read *Rhythm* to divert her thoughts. Vincy had brought it to convert her to Post-Impressionism.

When Archie and Dilly were out, and Edith, who always got up rather early, was alone, she often passed her morning hours in reading, dreaming, playing the piano, or even in thinking. She was one of the few women who really can think, and enjoy it. This morning she soon put down the mad clever little prophetic Oxford journal. Considering she was usually the most reposeful woman in London, she was rather restless today. She glanced round the little room;

there was nothing in it to distract or irritate, or even to suggest a train of thought; except perhaps the books; everything was calming and soothing, with a touch of gaiety in the lightness of the wall decorations. An azalea, certainly, would be a good note. The carpet, and almost everything in the room, was green, except the small white enamelled piano. Today she felt that she wanted to use all her influence to get Aylmer to confide in her more. Perhaps he was slipping away from her—she would have been only a little incident in his existence—while she certainly wished it to go on. Seeing this, perhaps it oughtn't to go on. She wondered if he would laugh or be serious today . . . whether . . .

Miss Bennett had come up in the lift with a heap of cardboard boxes, and the azalea. A taxi was waiting at the door.

Edith opened the boxes, cutting the string with scissors. She put four gowns out on the sofa. Grace explained that two were cloaks, two were gowns—all she could get.

'That's the one,' said Edith, taking out one of a deep blue colour, like an Italian sky on a coloured picture post-card. It had a collar of the same deep blue, spotted with white—a birdseye effect. Taking off her coat Edith slipped the gown over her dress, and went to her room (followed closely by Miss Bennett) to see herself in the long mirror.

'Perfect!' said Edith. 'Only I must cut off those buttons. I hate buttons.'

'How are you going to fasten it, then, dear?'

'With hooks and eyes. Marie can sew them on.'

The deep blue with the white spots had a vivid and charming effect, and suited her blonde colouring; she saw she was very pretty in it, and was pleased.

'Aren't you going to try the others on, dear?' asked Grace.

'No; what's the good? This one will do.'

'Right. Then I'll take them back.'

'You're sweet. Won't you come back to lunch?'

'I'll come back to lunch tomorrow,' said Miss Bennett, 'and you can tell me about your tea-party. Oh, and here's a little bit of stuff for the plant. I suppose you'll put the azalea into the large pewter vase?'

'Yes, and I'll tie this round its neck.'

'Sorry it's cotton,' said Miss Bennett. 'I couldn't get any silk the right colour.'

'Oh, I like cotton, if only it's not called sateen! Goodbye, darling. You're delightfully quick!'

'Yes, I don't waste time,' said Miss Bennett. 'Mother says, too, that I'm the best shopper in the world.' She turned round to add, 'I'm dying to know why you want to look so pretty. Who is it?'

With a quiet smile, Edith dismissed her.

24 Coming Up for Air

From *Dangerous Ages*

by Rose Macaulay

Rose Macaulay was born in the latter quarter of the nineteenth century in Cambridge and spent most of her childhood in Italy. Her first novel to attract notice was Potterism, *1920.* Dangerous Ages *was published in 1921 and others amongst many are* Told by an Idiot, *1923,* Orphan Island, *1924,* Crewe Train, *1929,* Keeping Up Appearances, *1928,* Staying with Relations, *1930.* The World My Wilderness, *1950, and* The Towers of Trebizond, *1956. She was also a great traveller (*Fabled Shore *is about the coast of Spain) and the author of biography and criticism. She was an extremely witty satirist. Since her death in 1958 many of her letters have been published.*

'Yes. It's this ridiculous work of hers. It's so absurd: a married woman of her age making her head ache working for examinations.'

In old days Jim and Neville had worked together. Jim had been proud of Neville's success; she had been quicker than he. Mrs. Hilary, who had welcomed Neville's marriage as ending all that, foresaw a renewal of the hurtful business.

But Jim looked grave and disapproving over it.

'It is absurd,' he agreed, and her heart rose. 'And of course she can't do it, can't make up all that leeway. Besides her brain has lost its grip. She's not kept it sharpened; she's spent her life on people. You can't have it both ways—a woman can't, I mean. Her work's been different. She doesn't seem to realise that what she's trying to learn up again now, in the spare moments of an already full life, demands a whole lifetime of hard work. She can't get back those twenty years; no one could. And she can't get back the clear, gripping brain she had before she had children. She's given some of it to them. That's nature's way, unfortunately. Hard luck, no doubt, but there it is; you can't get round it. Nature's a hybrid of fool and devil.'

He was talking really to himself, but was recalled to his mother by the tears which, he suddenly perceived, were distorting her face.

'And so,' she whispered, her voice choked, 'we women get left. . . .'

He looked away from her, a little exasperated. She cried so easily and so superfluously, and he knew that these tears were more for herself than for Neville. And she didn't really come into what he had been saying at all; he had been talking about brains.

'It's all right as far as most women are concerned,' he said. 'Most women have no brains to be spoilt. Neville had. Most women could do nothing at all with life if they didn't produce children; it's their only possible job. *They've* no call to feel ill-used.'

25 Bird in a Cage

From *A Doll's House*

by Henrik Ibsen

Henrik Ibsen (1828–1906) was a Norwegian dramatist whose most famous plays dealt with social and psychological problems and were extremely advanced for their day. (Peer Gynt, 1866, is however, a lyrical drama). Ibsen was particularly eager to tear down the shams and conventions which prevented women from being themselves.

A Doll's House (the realization of a young wife that she has never been a person in her own right) was written in 1879, Ghosts in 1881, The Wild Duck in 1884, Rosmersholm in 1886, Hedda Gabler in 1890 and The Master Builder in 1892.

Nora: Sit down, Torvald; you and I have much to say to each other. *(She sits at one side of the table).*
Helmer: Nora—what does this mean? Your cold, set face—
Nora: Sit down. It will take some time. I have much to talk over with you.
(Helmer sits at the other side of the table).
Helmer: You alarm me, Nora. I don't understand you.
Nora: No, that is just it. You don't understand me; and I have never understood you—till tonight. No, don't interrupt. Only listen to what I say. We must come to a final settlement, Torvald.
Helmer: How do you mean?
Nora: (After a short silence) Does not one thing strike you as we sit here?
Helmer: What should strike me?
Nora: We have been married eight years. Does it not strike

you that this is the first time we two, you and I, man and wife, have talked together seriously?
Helmer: Seriously! What do you call seriously?
Nora: During eight whole years, and more—ever since the day we first met—we have never exchanged one serious word about serious things.
Helmer: Was I always to trouble you with the cares you could not help me to bear?
Nora: I am not talking of cares. I say that we have never yet set ourselves seriously to get to the bottom of anything.
Helmer. Why, my dearest Nora, what have you to do with serious things?
Nora: There we have it! You have never understood me—I have had great injustice done to me, Torvald; first by father, and then by you.
Helmer: What! By your father and me? By us, who have loved you more than all the world?
Nora: (Shaking her head) You have never loved me. You only thought it amusing to be in love with me.
Helmer: Why, Nora, what a thing to say.
Nora: Yes, it is so, Torvald. While I was at home with father, he used to tell me all his opinions, and I held the same opinions. If I had others, I said nothing about them, because he wouldn't have liked it. He used to call me his doll-child, and played with me as I played with my dolls. Then I came to live in your house—
Helmer: What an expression to use about our marriage!
Nora: (Undisturbed) I mean I passed from father's hands into yours. You arranged everything according to your taste; and I got the same tastes as you; or I pretended to—I don't know which—both ways, perhaps; sometimes one and sometimes the other. When I look back on it now, I seem to have been living here like a beggar, from hand to mouth. I lived by performing tricks for you, Torvald. But you would have it so. You and father have done me a great wrong. It is your fault that my life has come to nothing.
Helmer: Why, Nora, how unreasonable and ungrateful you are! Have you not been happy here?

Nora: No, never. I thought I was; but I never was.

Helmer: Not—not happy!

Nora: No; only merry. And you have always been so kind to me. But our house has been nothing but a play-room. Here I have been your doll-wife, just as at home I used to be papa's doll-child. And the children, in their turn, have been my dolls. I thought it fun when you played with me, just as the children did when I played with them. That has been our marriage, Torvald.

Helmer: There is some truth in what you say, exaggerated and over-strained though it be. But henceforth it shall be different. Play-time is over; now comes the time for education.

Nora: Whose education? Mine or the children's?

Helmer: Both, my dear Nora.

Nora: Oh, Torvald, you are not the man to teach me to be a fit wife for you.

Helmer: And you can say that?

Nora: And I—how have I prepared myself to educate the children?

Helmer: Nora!

Nora: Did you not say yourself, a few minutes ago, you dared not trust them to me?

Helmer: In the excitement of the moment! Why should you dwell upon that?

Nora: No—you were perfectly right. That problem is beyond me. There is another to be solved first—I must try to educate myself. You are not the man to help me in that. I must set about it alone. And that is why I am leaving you.

Helmer: (Jumping up) What—do you mean to say—?

Nora: I must stand quite alone if I am ever to know myself and my surroundings; so I cannot stay with you.

Helmer: Nora! Nora!

Nora: I am going at once. I daresay Christina will take me in for tonight.

Helmer: You are mad! I shall not allow it! I forbid it!

Nora: It is of no use your forbidding me anything now. I shall take with me what belongs to me. From you, I will accept nothing, either now or afterwards.

Helmer: What madness this is!

Nora: Tomorrow I shall go home—I mean to what was my home. It will be easier for me to find some opening there.
Helmer: Oh, in your blind inexperience—
Nora: I must try to gain experience, Torvald.
Helmer: To forsake your home, your husband, and your children! And you don't consider what the world will say.
Nora: I can pay no heed to that. I only know that I must do it.
Helmer: This is monstrous! Can you forsake your holiest duties in this way?
Nora: What do you consider my holiest duties?
Helmer: Do I need to tell you that? Your duties to your husband and your children.
Nora: I have other duties equally sacred.
Helmer: Impossible! What duties do you mean?
Nora: My duties towards myself.
Helmer: Before all else you are a wife and a mother.
Nora: That I no longer believe. I believe that before all else I am a human being, just as much as you are—or at least that I should try to become one. I know that most people agree with you, Torvald, and that they say so in books. But henceforth I can't be satisfied with what most people say, and what is in books. I must think things out for myself, and try to get clear about them.

26 Being an Outsider

From *The Holiday*

by Stevie Smith

Stevie Smith was born in Hull. Her first novel A Novel on Yellow Paper *was published in 1936 and* The Holiday *in 1949. She is a poet who often illustrates her own poems, e.g. 'Not Waving But Drowning' (1957). She is a true original and it is very difficult to convey the quiddity of her writing.*

So with these happy thoughts in my mind, I go down to out butcher, with whom my Aunt has dealt for forty years, and Mr. Montgomery the butcher gives me six ounces more than the ration book says. He is a tall thin man, looking like Charles II, he smiles as he wraps the parcel. There you are, my dear. How's Mother? (for he is convinced that my Aunt is my mother).

My mother died when I was a child, my Aunt has always lived with us, she has never wished to marry, she has 'no patience' with men (she also had 'no patience' with Hitler). She thinks men are soppy, she says: He is a very soppy man, a most soppy individual.

I love my Aunt, I love her, I love the life in the family, my familiar life, but I like also to go out and to see how the other people get along, and especially I like to see how the married ladies get along, and I sit and listen and watch, and I see how much they think about their husbands, even if they hate 'em like hell there is this thought, this attention.

How can you keep it up, Maria? I ask the women friends, I think you are absolutely marvellous to keep on thinking about them and listening to them and having the children and keeping the house going on turning round the men. I have never had such a thing heigh-ho.

And they are at first immensely pleased about this that I have been saying, but then they begin to wish not to stress how martyr-like wonderful it is, and they begin to say how much one is missing if one does not have it; so I have had trouble with my married women friends, and with those who are living free-like and unmarried with their darling chosen one, I have had trouble for two reasons, because sometimes I like the chosen-one too much, but mostly and the most trouble, because I do not like him enough, and because I think it is so wonderful of the women to be so unselfish and so kind. But I can see that they have to do it, if they are going to have a darling husband and a darling home of their own and darling children, they have to do it, there is no other way, and if you do not then you will live lonely and grow up to old solitude. Amen.

But most women, especially in the lower and lower-middle classes, are conditioned early to having 'father' the centre of the home-life, with father's chair, and father's dinner, and father's *Times* and father says, so they are not brought up like me to be this wicked selfish creature, to have no boring old father-talk, to have no papa at all that one attends to, to have a darling Aunt to come home to, that one admires, that is strong, happy, simple, shrewd, staunch, loving, upright and bossy, to have a darling sister that is working away from home, and to be for my Aunt, with this sister, the one.

27 Being Dissatisfied with the Love of Man

From *The Echoing Grove*

by Rosamond Lehmann

Rosamond Lehmann was a scholar at Girton College, Cambridge and her first novel published in 1927, Dusty Answer, *is partly set there. Some others are* The Weather in the Streets, *1936,* The Ballad and the Source, *1944, and* The Echoing Grove, *1953. She is also regarded, like Elizabeth Bowen, as a novelist of 'feminine sensibility' and it may be true that she appeals mainly to women.*

'He said he still loved me.'

'I expect he means it.'

'Then how can he . . . ? We were so happy—not always, but most of the time, as he agrees. Do I understand *nothing*? He says I don't. Does it always wear out? Are men bound to get sick of making love to the same woman, even if it's—if it seems to her—very successful? Is that all there is to it?'

Glancing at the childishly quivering face, Dinah said with pity and kindness:

'It's not all there is to it by any means; but it does seem almost insoluble. I can't help thinking it's particularly difficult to be a woman just at present. One feels so transitional and fluctuating . . . So I suppose do men. I believe we *are* all in flux—that the difference between our grandmothers and us is far deeper than we realise—much more fundamental than the obvious social economic one. Our so-called emancipation may be a symptom, not a cause. Sometimes I think it's more than the development of a new attitude towards sex: that a new gender may be evolving—psychically new—a sort of hybrid. Or else it's just beginning to be uncovered how much woman there is in man and *vice versa*.' She pondered. 'Perhaps when we understand more, unearth more of what goes on in the unconscious, we shall manage to behave better to one another. It's ourselves we're trying to destroy when we're destructive: at least I think that explains the people who never can sustain a human relationship. It's not good and evil struggling in them: it's the suppressed unaccepted unacceptable man or woman in them they have to cast out . . . can't come to terms with.'

28 Being a Sensitive Soul

From *Howards End*

by E. M. Forster

E. M. Forster was born in 1879 and has written only five novels (all between 1905 and 1924) of which the best-known is the last, A Passage to India. Howards End points up the differences between two ways of life, the imaginative and idealistic and the philistine and conventional, typified by the Schlegels and the Wilcoxes. After violent events some sort of compromise is reached but the argument can never be resolved. Forster is also a critic and essayist.

'You shall see the connection if it kills you, Henry! You have had a mistress—I forgave you. My sister has a lover—you drive her from the house. Do you see the connection? Stupid, hypocritical, cruel—oh, contemptible!—a man who insults his wife when she's alive and cants with her memory when she's dead. A man who ruins a woman for his pleasure, and casts her off to ruin other men. And gives bad financial advice, and then says he is not responsible. These men are you. You can't recognise them, because you can't connect. I've had enough of your unneeded kindness. I've spoilt you long enough. All your life you have been spoiled. Mrs. Wilcox spoiled you. No one has ever told you what you are—muddled, criminally muddled. Men like you use repentance as a blind, so don't repent. Only say to yourself, "What Helen has done, I've done".'

'The two cases are different,' Henry stammered. His real retort was not quite ready. His brain was still in a whirl, and he wanted a little longer.

'In what way different? You have betrayed Mrs. Wilcox,

Helen only herself. You remain in society, Helen can't. You have had only pleasure, she may die. You have the insolence to talk to me of differences, Henry?'

Oh, the uselessness of it! Henry's retort came.

'I perceive you are attempting blackmail. It is scarcely a pretty weapon for a wife to use against her husband. My rule through life has been never to pay the least attention to threats, and I can only repeat what I have said before. I do not give you and your sister leave to sleep at Howards End.'

Margaret loosed his hands. He went into the house, wiping first one and then the other on his handkerchief. For a little she stood looking at the Six Hills, tombs of warriors, breasts of the spring. Then she passed out into what was now the evening.

29 Loving

From *The Woodlanders*

by Thomas Hardy

Thomas Hardy (1840–1928) was born the son of a builder in Dorchester and was an architect in his youth. Most of his works are set in nineteenth century 'Wessex' (Dorset and its adjoining counties). Hardy also wrote a long epic poem 'The Dynasts' and was a very great lyric poet.

'Nature' in his novels is indifferent to struggling humanity but his underlying pessimism is lightened by a rich vein of humour. His best known novels are Under the Greenwood Tree, 1872, Far From The Madding Crowd, 1874, The Return of the Native, 1878, The Mayor of Casterbridge, 1866, The Woodlanders, 1887, Tess of the D'Urbervilles, 1891, *and* Jude the Obscure, 1896. *The latter contains the portrait of the 'progressive woman' of that time. The Woodlanders, from which the following extract is taken is an altogether gentler book.*

It was Marty, as they had supposed. That evening had been the particular one of the week upon which Grace and herself had been accustomed to privately deposit flowers on Giles's grave, and this was the first occasion since his death eight months earlier on which Grace had failed to keep her appointment. Mary had waited in the road just outside Melbury's, where her fellow-pilgrim had been wont to join her, till she was weary; and at last, thinking that Grace had missed her, and gone on alone, she followed the way to the church, but saw no Grace in front of her. It got later, and Marty continued her walk till she reached the churchyard gate; but still no Grace. Yet her sense of comradeship would not allow her to go on to the grave alone, and still thinking the delay had been unavoidable, she stood there with her little basket of flowers in her clasped hands, and her feet chilled by the damp ground, till more than two hours had passed. She then heard the footsteps of the search. In the silence of the night Marty could not help Melbury's men, who presently passed on their return from hearing fragments of their conversation, from which she acquired a general idea of what had occurred, and where Mrs. Fitzpiers then was.

Immediately they had dropped down the hill she entered the churchyard, going to a secluded corner behind the bushes, where rose the unadorned stone that marked the last bed of Giles Winterborne. As this solitary and silent girl stood there in the moonlight, a straight slim figure, clothed in a plaitless gown, the contours of womanhood so undeveloped as to be scarcely perceptible, the marks of poverty and toil effaced by the misty hour, she touched sublimity at points, and looked almost like a being who had rejected with indifference the attribute of sex for the loftier quality of abstract humanism. She stooped down and cleared away the withered flowers that Grace and herself had laid there the previous week, and put her fresh ones in their place.

'Now, my own, own love,' she whispered, 'you are mine, and on'y mine; for she has forgot 'ee at last, although for her you died! But I—whenever I get up I'll think of 'ee, and whenever I lie down I'll think of 'ee. Whenever I plant the young larches I'll think that none can plant as you planted; and whenever I split a gad, and whenever I turn the cider wring, I'll say none could do it like you. If ever I forget your name let me forget home and heaven! . . . But no, no, my love, I never can forget 'ee; for you was a good man, and did good things!'

30 Being in Love II

From *Letters to Imlay*

by Mary Wollstonecraft

Mary Wollstonecraft met the handsome American Captain Gilbert Imlay after she went to Paris in 1792. She was deeply in love with him and bore him a daughter, Fanny. Her personal life was both enriched and ruined by him. In fact she attempted suicide after he abandoned her. Six months after her final breach with Imlay she had committed herself to William Godwin, for her nature yearned for security and permanency. Imlay was absent on business in Le Havre for some months in 1793 and 1794 and it was during this period that her letters to him began. She joined him in February 1794 and Fanny was born in April 1794. After this there were many long separations before their final separation in 1796.

If you are interested in the life of Mary Wollstonecraft, the introduction to the Letters to Imlay *by C. Kegan Paul (1879) is very informative and sympathetic. Her second husband, William Godwin, also wrote a biography of her.*

(Hull, 1795)
Friday, June 12.

I have just received yours dated the 9th, which I suppose was a mistake, for it could scarcely have loitered so long on the road. The general observations which apply to the state of your own mind, appear to me just, as far as they go; and I shall always consider it as one of the most serious misfortunes of my life, that I did not meet you, before satiety had rendered your senses so fastidious, as almost to close up every tender avenue of sentiment and affection that leads to your sympathetic heart. You have a heart my friend, yet, hurried away by the impetuosity of inferior feelings, you have sought in vulgar excesses for that gratification which only the heart can bestow.

The common run of men, I know, with strong health and gross appetites, must have variety to banish *ennui*, because the imagination never lends its magic wand, to convert appetite into love, cemented by according reason. Ah! my friend, you know not the ineffable delight, the exquisite pleasure, which arises from an unison of affection and desire, when the whole soul and senses are abandoned to a lively imagination, that renders every emotion delicate and rapturous. Yes; these are emotions, over which satiety has no power, and the recollection of which, even disappointment cannot disenchant; but they do not exist without self-denial. These emotions, more or less strong, appear to me to be the distinctive characteristic of genius, the foundation of taste, and of that exquisite relish for the beauties of nature, of which the common herd of eaters and drinkers and *child-begetters* certainly have no idea. You will smile at an observation that has just occurred to me:—I consider these minds as the most strong and original whose imagination acts as the stimulus to their senses.

Well! you will ask what is the result of all this reasoning? Why, I cannot help thinking that it is possible for you, having great strength of mind, to return to nature, and regain a sanity of constitution, and purity of feeling, which would open your heart to me. I would fain rest there!

Yet, convinced more than ever of the sincerity and tenderness of my attachment to you, the involuntary hopes which a determination to live has revived, are not sufficiently strong to dissipate the cloud that despair has spread over futurity. I have looked at the sea, and at my child, hardly daring to own to myself the secret wish, that it might become our tomb; and that the heart, still so alive to anguish, might there be quieted by death. At this moment ten thousand complicated sentiments press for utterance, weigh on my heart, and obscure my sight.

Are we ever to meet again? and will you endeavour to render that meeting happier than the last? Will you endeavour to restrain your caprices, in order to give vigour to affection, and to give play to the checked sentiments that nature intended should expand your heart? I cannot indeed, without agony, think of your bosom's being continually contaminated; and bitter are the tears which exhaust my eyes, when I recollect why my child and I are forced to stray from the asylum, in which, after so many storms, I had hoped to rest, smiling at angry fate. These are not common sorrows; nor can you perhaps conceive how much active fortitude it requires to labour perpetually to blunt the shafts of disappointment.

Examine now yourself, and ascertain whether you can live in something like a settled style. Let our confidence in future be unbounded; consider whether you find it necessary to sacrifice me to what you term 'the zest of life'; and, when you have once a clear view of your own motives, of your own incentive to action, do not deceive me!

The train of thoughts which the writing of this epistle awoke, makes me so wretched that I must take a walk, to rouse and calm my mind. But first, let me tell you, that, if you really wish to promote my happiness, you will endeavour to give me as much as you can of yourself. You have great mental energy, and your judgment seems to me so just that it is only the dupe of your inclination in discussing one subject.

The post does not go out today. Tomorrow I may write more tranquilly. I cannot yet say when the vessel will sail in which I have determined to depart.

31 Man's Ideal Wife—and Later

From *Middlemarch*

by George Eliot

See under Extract No. 12 for notes on George Eliot.

Dr. Lydgate has fallen in love with Rosamond Vincy and believes she will be an ideal wife for him. Rosamond is pretty and loving but very attached to the material things of life. Lack of money leads the household into debt and Rosamond is extravagant. She is also a snob and cares more for giving a good impression in provincial society than for her husband's happiness. She loses her first baby. Slowly the husband and wife become alienated. Lydgate is scientifically ambitious and Rosamond has no interest in his career apart from the position it brings her.

He touched her ear and a little bit of neck under it with his lips, and they sat quite still for many minutes which flowed by them like a small gurgling brook with the kisses of the sun upon it. Rosamond thought that no one could be more in love than she was; and Lydgate thought that after all his wild mistakes and absurd credulity, he had found perfect womanhood—felt as if already breathed upon by exquisite wedded affection such as would be bestowed by an accomplished creature who venerated his high musings and momentous labours and would never interfere with them; who would create order in the home and accounts with still magic, yet keep her fingers ready to touch the lute and transform life into romance at any moment; who was instructed to the true womanly limit and not a hair's breadth beyond—docile, therefore, and ready to carry out behests which came from beyond that limit. It was plainer now than ever that his notion of remaining much longer a bachelor had been a mistake: marriage would not be an obstruction but a furtherance. And happening the next day to accompany a patient to Brassing, he saw a dinner-service there which struck him as so exactly the right thing that he bought it at once. It saved time to do these things just when you thought of them, and Lydgate hated ugly crockery. The dinner-service in question was expensive, but that that might be in the nature of dinner-services. Furnishing was necessarily expensive; but then it had to be done only once.

* * *

In spite of Rosamond's self-control a tear fell silently and rolled over her lips. She still said nothing; but under that quietude was hidden an intense effect: she was in such entire disgust with her husband that she wished that she had never seen him. Sir Godwin's rudeness towards her and utter want of feeling ranged him with Dover and all other creditors—disagreeable people who only thought of themselves, and did not mind how annoying they were to her. Even her father was unkind, and might have done more for them. In fact there was but one person in Rosamond's world whom she did not regard as blameworthy, and that was the graceful creature with blond plaits and with little hands crossed before her, who had never expressed herself unbecomingly, and had always acted for the best—the best naturally being what she best liked.

Lydgate pausing and looking at her again began to feel that half-maddening sense of helplessness which comes over passionate people when their passion is met by an innocent-looking silence whose meek victimised air seems to put them in the wrong, and at last infects even the justest indignation with a doubt of its justice. He needed to recover the full sense that he was in the right by moderating his words.

'Can you not see, Rosamond,' he began again, trying to be simply grave and not bitter, 'that nothing can be so fatal as a want of openness and confidence between us? It has happened again and again that I have expressed a decided wish, and you have seemed to assent, yet after that you have secretly disobeyed my wish. In that way I can never know what I have to trust to. There would be some hope for us if you would admit this. Am I such an unreasonable, furious brute? Why should you not be open with me?'

Still silence.

'Will you only say that you have been mistaken, and that I may depend on your not acting secretly in future?' said Lydgate, urgently, but with something of request in his tone which Rosamond was quick to perceive. She spoke with coolness.

'I cannot possibly make admissions or promises in answer to such words as you have used towards me. I have not been accustomed to language of that kind. You have spoken of my "secret meddling," and my "interfering ignorance," and my "false assent." I have never expressed myself in that way to you, and I think that you ought to apologise. You spoke of its being impossible to live with me. Certainly you have not made my life pleasant to me of late. I think it was to be expected that I should try to avert some of the hardships which our marriage has brought on me.' Another tear fell as Rosamond ceased speaking, and she pressed it away as quietly as the first.

Lydgate flung himself into a chair, feeling checkmated. What place was there in her mind for a remonstrance to lodge in? He laid down his hat, flung an arm over the back of his chair, and looked down for some moments without speaking. Rosamond had the double purchase over him of insensibility to the point of justice in his reproach, and of sensibility to the undeniable hardships now present in her married life. Although her duplicity in the affair of the house had exceeded what he knew, and had really hindered the Plymdales from knowing of it, she had no consciousness that her action could rightly be called false. We are not obliged to identify our own acts according to a strict classification, any more than the materials of our grocery and clothes. Rosamond felt that she was aggrieved, and that was what Lydgate had to recognise.

As for him, the need of accommodating himself to her nature, which was inflexible in proportion to its negations, held him as with pincers. He had begun to have an alarmed foresight of her irrevocable loss of love for him, and the consequent dreariness of their life. The ready fulness of his emotions made this dread alternate quickly with the first violent movements of his anger. It would assuredly have been a vain boast in him to say that he was her master.

'You have not made my life pleasant to me of late'—'the hardships which our marriage has brought on me'—these words were stinging his imagination as a pain makes an exaggerated dream. If he were not only to sink from his highest resolve, but to sink into the hideous fettering of domestic hate?

'Rosamond,' he said, turning his eyes on her with a melancholy look, 'you should allow for a man's words when he is disappointed and provoked. You and I cannot have opposite interests. I cannot part my happiness from yours. If I am angry with you, it is that you seem not to see how any concealment divides us. How could I wish to make anything hard to you either by my words or conduct? When I hurt you, I hurt part of my own life. I should never be angry with you if you would be quite open with me.'

'I have only wished to prevent you from hurrying us into wretchedness without any necessity,' said Rosamond, the tears coming again from a softened feeling now that her husband had softened. 'It is so very hard to be disgraced here among all the people we know, and to live in such a miserable way. I wish I had died with the baby.'

She spoke and wept with that gentleness which makes such words and tears omnipotent over a loving-hearted man. Lydgate drew his chair near to hers and pressed her delicate head against his cheek with his powerful tender hand. He only caressed her; he did not say anything; for what was there to say? He could not promise to shield her from that dreaded wretchedness, for he could see no sure means of doing so. When he left her to go out again, he told himself that it was ten times harder for her than for him: he had a life away from home, and constant appeals to his activity on behalf of others. He wished to excuse everything in her if he could—but it was inevitable that in that excusing mood he should think of her as if she were an animal of another and feebler species. Nevertheless she had mastered him.

32 Man's Ideal of Woman

From *An Ideal Husband*

by Oscar Wilde

Oscar Wilde (1854–1900) was a famous wit and conversationalist and the author of the story The Picture of Dorian Gray, *1891, and the plays* Lady Windermere's Fan, *1892,* An Ideal Husband, *1895 and* The Importance of Being Earnest, *1895, among others. In the same year he was sentenced to imprisonment for homosexual offences. He was a great friend of Ada Leverson q.v. page 80.*

Lord Goring (Pulling himself together for a great effort and showing the philosophy that underlies the dandy): Lady Chiltern, allow me. You wrote me a letter last night in which you said you trusted me and wanted my help. Now is the moment when you really want my help, now is the time when you have got to trust me, to trust in my counsel and judgment. You love Robert. Do you want to kill his love for you? What sort of existence will he have if you rob him of the fruits of his ambition? If you take him from the splendour of a great political career, if you close the doors of public life against him, if you condemn him to sterile failure, he who was made for triumph and success? Women are not meant to judge us, but to forgive us when we need forgiveness. Pardon, not punishment, is their mission. Why should you scourge him with rods for a sin done in his youth, before he knew you, before he knew himself? A man's life is of more value than a woman's. It has larger issues, wider scope, greater ambitions. A woman's life revolves in curves of emotions. It is upon lines of intellect that a man's life progresses. Don't make any terrible mistake, Lady Chiltern. A woman who can keep

a man's love, and love him in return, has done all the world wants of women, and should want of them.
Lady Chiltern (Troubled and hesitating): But it is my husband himself who wishes to retire from public life. He feels it is his duty. It was he who first said so.
Lord Goring: Rather than lose your love, Robert would do anything, wreck his whole career, as he is on the brink of doing now. He is making for you a terrible sacrifice. Take my advice, Lady Chiltern, and do not accept a sacrifice so great. If you do, you will live to repent it bitterly. We men and women are not made to accept such sacrifices from each other. We are not worthy of them. Besides, Robert has been punished enough.

33 Woman Playing Up to Her Role

From *An Ideal Husband*

by Oscar Wilde

See under Extract No. 32 for notes on Oscar Wilde.

Sir Robert Chiltern (Bowing): Everybody is dying to know the brilliant Mrs. Cheveley. Our attachés at Vienna write to us about nothing else.
Mrs. Cheveley: Thank you, Sir Robert. An acquaintance that begins with a compliment is sure to develop into a real friendship. It starts in the right manner. And I find that I know Lady Chiltern already.
Sir Robert Chiltern: Really?
Mrs. Cheveley: Yes. She has just reminded me that we were at school together. I remember it perfectly now. She always got the good conduct prize. I have a distinct recollection of Lady Chiltern always getting the good conduct prize.
Sir Robert Chiltern (Smiling): And what prizes did you get, Mrs. Cheveley?
Mrs. Cheveley: My prizes came a little later on in life. I don't think any of them were for good conduct. I forget!
Sir Robert Chiltern: I am sure they were for something charming!
Mrs. Cheveley: I don't know that women are always rewarded for being charming. I think they are usually punished for it! Certainly, more women grow old nowadays through the faithfulness of their admirers than through anything else! At least that is the only way I can account for the terribly haggard look of your pretty women in London.
Sir Robert Chiltern: What an appalling philosophy that

sounds! To attempt to classify you, Mrs. Cheveley, would be an impertinence. But may I ask, at heart, are you an optimist or a pessimist? These seem to be the only two fashionable religions left to us nowadays.
Mrs. Cheveley: Oh, I'm neither. Optimism begins in a broad grin, and pessimism ends with blue spectacles. Besides, they are both of them merely poses.
Sir Robert Chiltern: You prefer to be natural?
Mrs. Cheveley: Sometimes. But it is such a very difficult pose to keep up.
Sir Robert Chiltern: What would those modern psychological novelists, of whom we hear so much, say to such a theory as that?
Mrs. Cheveley: Ah! The strength of women comes from the fact that psychology cannot explain us. Men can be analysed, women . . . merely adored.
Sir Robert Chiltern: You think science cannot grapple with the problem of women?
Mrs. Cheveley: Science can never grapple with the irrational. That is why it has no future before it, in this world.
Sir Robert Chiltern; And women represent the irrational.
Mrs. Cheveley: Well-dressed women do.
Sir Robert Chiltern (*With a polite bow*): I fear I could hardly agree with you there. But do sit down. And now tell me, what makes you leave your brilliant Vienna for our gloomy London—or perhaps the question is indiscreet?
Mrs. Cheveley: Questions are never indiscreet. Answers sometimes are.
Sir Robert Chiltern: Well, at any rate, may I know if it is politics or pleasure?
Mrs. Cheveley: Politics are my only pleasure. You see nowadays it is not fashionable to flirt till one is forty, or to be romantic till one is forty-five, so we poor women who are under thirty, or say we are, having nothing open to us but politics or philanthropy. And philanthropy seems to me to have become simply the refuge of people who wish to annoy their fellow-creatures. I prefer politics. I think they are more . . . becoming!

34 The Shavian Ideal of Woman and Man

From *Man and Superman*

by George Bernard Shaw

George Bernard Shaw (1856–1950) was an Irishman, early Fabian, music-critic and dramatist. His best-known works are Man and Superman, Saint Joan, Candida, You Never Can Tell, Mrs. Warren's Profession *and* The Apple Cart. *The prefaces to his plays are works in themselves. He was undoubtedly influenced by Ibsen but had a powerful personality with decided views on politics and economics. Read* The Intelligent Woman's Guide to Socialism and Capitalism. *In* Man and Superman *two of his major themes —the life force and the power of woman over man are to the fore.*

Tanner: Tavy: that's the devilish side of a woman's fascination: she makes you will your own destruction.

Octavius: But it's not destruction: it's fulfilment.

Tanner: Yes, of her purpose; and that purpose is neither her happiness nor yours, but Nature's. Vitality in a woman is a blind fury of creation. She sacrifices herself to it: Do you think she will hesitate to sacrifice you?

Octavius: Why, it is just because she is self-sacrificing that she will not sacrifice those she loves.

Tanner: That is the profoundest of mistakes, Tavy. It is the self-sacrificing women that sacrifice others most recklessly. Because they are unselfish, they are kind in little things. Because they have a purpose which is not their own purpose, but that of the whole universe, a man is nothing to them but the instrument of that purpose.

Octavius: Don't be ungenerous, Jack. They take the tenderest care of us.

Tanner: Yes, as a soldier takes care of his rifle or a musician of his violin. But do they allow us any purpose or freedom of our own? Will they lend us to one another? Can the strongest man escape from them when once he is appropriated? They tremble when we are in danger, and weep when we die; but the tears are not for us, but for a father wasted, a son's breeding thrown away. They accuse us of treating them as a mere means to our pleasure; but how can so feeble and transient a folly as a man's selfish pleasure enslave a woman as the whole purpose of Nature embodied in a woman can enslave a man?
Octavius: What matter, if the slavery makes us happy?
Tanner: No matter at all if you have no purpose of your own, and are, like most men, a mere breadwinner. But you, Tavy, are an artist: that is you have a purpose as absorbing and as unscrupulous as a woman's purpose.
Octavius: Not unscrupulous.
Tanner: Quite unscrupulous. The true artist will let his wife starve, his children go barefoot, his mother drudge for his living at seventy, sooner than work at anything but his art. To women he is half-vivisector, half-vampire. He gets into intimate relations with them to study them, to strip the mask of convention from them, to surprise their inmost secrets, knowing that they have the power to rouse his deepest creative energies, to rescue him from his cold reason, to make him see visions and dream dreams, to inspire him, as he calls it. He persuades women that they may do this for their own purpose whilst he really means them to do it for his. He steals the mother's milk and blackens it to make printers ink to scoff at her and glorify ideal women with. He pretends to spare her the pangs of childbearing so that he may have for himself the tenderness and fostering that belong of right to her children. Since marriage began, the great artist has been known as a bad husband. But he is worse: he is a child-robber, a bloodsucker, a hypocrite and a cheat. Perish the race and wither a thousand women if only the sacrifice of them enable him to act *Hamlet* better, to paint a finer picture, to write a deeper poem, a greater play, a profound philosophy! For mark you, Tavy, the artist's work is to shew us ourselves

as we really are. Our minds are nothing but this knowledge of ourselves; and he who adds a jot to such knowledge creates new mind as surely as any women creates new men. In the rage of that creation he is as ruthless as the woman, as dangerous to her as she is to him, and as horribly fascinmating. Of all human struggles there is none so treacherous and remorseless as the struggle between the artist man and the mother woman. Which shall use up the other? That is the issue between them. And it is all the deadlier because, in your romanticist cant, they love one another.
Octavius: Even if it were so—and I don't admit it for a moment—it is out of the deadliest struggles that we get the noblest characters.
Tanner: Remember that the next time you meet a grizzly bear or a Bengal tiger, Tavy.
Octavius: I meant where there is love, Jack.
Tanner: Oh, the tiger will love you. There is no love sincerer than the love of food. I think Ann loves you that way; she patted your cheek as if it were a nicely underdone chop.
Octavius: You know, Jack, I should have to run away from you if I did not make it a fixed rule not to mind anything you say. You come out with perfectly revolting things sometimes.

Act II

Tanner: You think that you are Ann's suitor; that you are the pursuer and she the pursued; that it is your part to woo, to persuade, to prevail, to overcome. Fool: it is you who are the pursued, the marked down quarry, the destined prey. You need not sit looking longingly at the bait through the wires of the trap; the door is open, and will remain so until it shuts behind you for ever.
Octavius: I wish I could believe that, vilely as you put it.
Tanner: Why, man, what other work has she in life but to get a husband? It is a woman's business to get married as soon as possible, and a man's to keep unmarried as long as he can. You have your poems and your tragedies to work at: Ann has nothing.

Octavius: I cannot write without inspiration. And nobody can give me that except Ann.

Tanner: Well, hadn't you better get it from her at a safer distance? Petrarch didn't see half as much of Laura, nor Dante of Beatrice, as you see of Ann now; and yet they wrote first-rate poetry—at least so I'm told. They never exposed their idolatry to the test of domestic familiarity; and it lasted them to their graves. Marry Ann; and at the end of a week you'll find no more inspiration in her than in a plate of muffins.

Octavius: You think I shall tire of her!

Tanner: Not at all: you don't get tired of muffins. But you don't find inspiration in them; and you won't in her when she ceases to be a poet's dream and becomes a solid eleven-stone wife. You'll be forced to dream about somebody else; and then there will be a row.

Octavius: This sort of talk is no use, Jack. You don't understand. You have never been in love.

Tanner: I! I have never been out of it. Why, I am in love even with Ann. But I am neither the slave of love nor its dupe. Go to the bee, thou poet: consider her ways and be wise. By heaven, Tavy, if women could do without our work and we ate their children's bread instead of making it, they would kill us as the spider kills her mate or as the bees kill the drone. And they would be right if we were good for nothing but love.

Octavius: Ah, if we were only good enough for love! There is nothing like love: there is nothing else but love: without it the world would be a dream of sordid horror.

Tanner: And this—*this* is the man who asks me to give him the hand of my ward! Tavy: I believe we were changed in our cradles, and that you are the real descendant of Don Juan.

Octavius: I beg you not to say anything like that to Ann.

Tanner: Don't be afraid. She has marked you for her own; and nothing will stop her now. You are doomed.

35 Being a 'Free' Woman

From *My Life*

by Isadora Duncan

Isadora Duncan (1878–1927) was a dancer born in San Francisco who developed her theories of interpretative dancing, based on Greek forms and modern aesthetic thought during her long residence in Europe. This was against the whole tradition of the ballet. She travelled all over the world with her school of children and was notorious for her free way of life. Her autobiography My Life, *1927, from which this extract is taken is noted for her frank revelations. Her children died in tragic circumstances and she herself died in a car accident in the South of France.*

I was so inexperienced as to think that having a baby was a perfectly natural process. I went to live in this villa, which was a hundred miles from any town, and I engaged a village doctor. In my ignorance, I was quite content to have this village doctor, who, I think, was only used to peasant women.

As I walked beside the sea, I sometimes felt an excess of strength and prowess, and I thought this creature would be mine, mine alone, but on other days, when the sky was grey and the cold North Sea waves were angry, I had sudden, sinking moods, when I felt myself some poor animal in a mighty trap, and I struggled with an overwhelming desire to escape, escape. Where? Perhaps even into the midst of the sullen waves. I struggled against such moods and bravely overcame them, nor did I ever let anyone suspect what I felt, but, nevertheless, such moods were waiting for me at odd hours, and were difficult to avoid. Also I thought that most people were receding from me. My mother seemed thousands of miles away. Craig was also strangely remote, and always immersed in his Art, whereas I could think less and less of my Art, and was only absorbed in this fearful, monstrous task which had fallen to me; this maddening joy-giving, pain-giving mystery.

How long and tortuous lagged the hours. The days, weeks, months, how slowly they passed! With alternate hope and despair, I often thought of the pilgrimage of my childhood, my youth, my wanderings in distant countries, my discoveries in Art, and they were as a misty, far-away prologue, leading up to this—the before-birth of a child. What any peasant woman could have! This was the culminating point of all my ambitions!

* * *

Ah, but the baby! The baby was astonishing; formed like a Cupid, with blue eyes and long brown hair, that afterwards fell out and gave place to golden curls. And miracle of miracles, that mouth sought my breast and bit with toothless gums, and pulled and drank the milk that gushed forth . . .

Oh, women, what is the good of us learning to become lawyers, painters, or sculptors, when this miracle exists? Now I knew this tremendous love, surpassing the love of man. I was stretched and bleeding, torn and helpless, while the little being sucked and howled. Life, life, life! Give me life! Oh, where was my Art? My Art or any Art? What did I care for Art? I felt I was a God, superior to any artist.

During the first weeks, I used to lie long hours with the baby in my arms, watching her asleep; sometimes catching a gaze from her eyes; feeling very near the edge, the mystery, perhaps the knowledge of life. This soul in the newly created body which answered my gaze with such apparently old eyes—the eyes of Eternity—gazing into mine with love. Love, perhaps, was the answer of all. What words could describe this joy? What wonder that I, who am not a writer, cannot find any words at all!

36 Bringing Up a Baby

From *A Proper Marriage*

by Doris Lessing

Doris Lessing was born in 1919. Her family lived in what was then Southern Rhodesia and she left that country in 1949. She has written of it in one of her best novels The Grass is Singing, *1950, and, in a series of novels whose heroine is Martha Quest, has explored the sexual and political growing up of Martha against a background of Rhodesian society. (*Martha Quest, *1952;* A Proper Marriage, *1954,* A Ripple from the Storm, *1958 and* Landlocked, *1965).* The Golden Notebook, *1962, tells a good deal about the plight of the 'emancipated' woman intellectual. She has written poems, many short stories and a play as well as novels but her main interests seem to be in social and political questions. Her best novels and stories, however, are straightforward and detailed evocations of people and places.*

Ever since that day Mr. Maynard had entered on the unpleasant scene of Caroline being fed, when Martha had seen it sharply through his eyes, she had forced herself, and with an effort that exhausted her, not to care about Caroline's eating. She must break this bond! That was how she felt; as something compulsive and deadly that would most certainly affect the child's whole future. So Martha no longer cared, on principle. But at the beginning it had not been so easy. She prepared the messes suitable for Caroline's age, set them on the wooden platform before the child, put a piece of linoleum under the high chair, and retired with a cup of tea and a book, forcing herself not to look at her.

And now what contests of will followed! Caroline had

been used to a forceful pillar of a mother standing over her with a glinting hard spoon full of stuff that she *must* eat, no matter how she tightened her lips and turned away her face; now she saw this same woman—and from one day to the next—sitting away from her on the other side of the room, not listening to her cries of rage and shrieks of defiance. Caroline picked up the bowl of porridge and flung it on the floor so that the greyish mess splashed everywhere —Martha turned a page and did not look. Caroline sparked her black eyes at Martha, let out short sharp cries of anger to *make* her look; then she picked up a mug of milk and poured it all over herself. Martha remained indifferent in her chair; but there was a tight-lipped tension about her that Caroline knew. She paddled her hands in a lake of soiled milk and rubbed them in her hair, singing out her defiance. And suddenly Martha became a whirlwind of exasperation. She jumped up and said despairingly: 'Oh Caroline you are a naughty, naughty girl!'

The little girl, with blobs of porridge on her face, her hair plastered and dripping with milk, gurgled out triumphant defiance. Then she found herself lifted roughly from the chair; she yelled angrily while Martha held her kicking under her arm, and bent to fill the bath. She was dropped into the water, soaped hastily, she felt herself whirled into new clean clothes, and then she was dropped into her wooden pen, where she soon forgot all about it, and began playing with her toys.

In the meantime Martha was scrubbing porridge and milk off the floor, the furniture, herself. She was sick with disgust at the mess. She was asking herself why she had endured months of that other mess, with only occasional lapses into distaste, a period when napkins, and then clothes and blankets had been wet and dirty, without difficulty. The book had said so. The book and she had been admirably justified; Caroline was now as the phrase went perfectly clean. But that had been no problem; the battle centred on food. What is it all about? asked Martha in despair. She was furious with herself for losing her temper. She could have wept with annoyance. She was saying to herself as she wiped off milk and grey pulp; Oh,

Lord how I hate this business, I do loathe it so. She was saying she hated her daughter; and she knew it. Soon the hot anger died; guilt unfailingly succeeded.

Outside, on the little verandah which was like a wired cage projecting out into the sunlight—the sun was now pouring down from over the trees in the park—Caroline was cheerfully gurgling and singing to herself. Inside the room, Martha was seated, tired and miserable. Her heart was now a hot enlarged area of tenderness for the child whom she was so lamentably mishandling.

She went out into the verandah. Caroline, in her short bright dress, looked up with her quick black eyes, and made an enquiring noise. She was snatched up and held against Martha's bosom. At once she began striving free: Martha laughed ruefully and put her down; she staggered around the room, singing to herself.

But she had eaten absolutely nothing. Martha produced rusks, and left them surreptitiously about the room— Caroline seized on them and began chewing vigorously.

'Oh Caroline!' sighed Martha, 'what am I going to do with you?'

She was forming the habit of talking to the child as if to herself. The small brain was receiving the sound of a half-humorous, resentful, grumbling, helpless voice rumbling away over her head.

'My poor unfortunate brat, what had you done to deserve a mother like me? Well, there's no help for it, you'll just have to put up with it. You bore me to extinction, and that's the truth of it, and no doubt I bore you. But as far as I can make out, one of the most important functions of parents is that they should be suitable objects of hate; if psychology doesn't mean that, it means nothing. Well then, so it's right and proper you should hate my guts off and on, you and I are just victims, my poor child, you can't help it, I can't help it, my mother couldn't help it and her mother . . .'

After a silence the voice went on, rather like Caroline's own meditative experimental rumblings and chirpings: 'So there we are, and we'd better make the best of it. As soon as possible I'll send you to a nursery school, where you are well out of my poisonous influence, I'll do that for you at least.'

By nine in the morning, it seemed always as if long stretches of the day had been lived through. And yet, it was three hours till lunchtime. Martha sewed—she and Caroline had dozens of those cheap pretty dresses. She watched the clock. She cooked the little messes for Caroline. She leafed hopefully through *the book*—or rather, whichever one of them seemed most likely to provide what she wanted, to see if she had overlooked some pattern of words that might help her to feel better. And at the least she felt she was being honest, that virtue which she was still convinced was the supreme one. Somewhere at the bottom of her heart was a pleasant self-righteousness that while she was as little fitted for maternity as her mother had been, she at least had the honesty to admit it.

She would watch lunchtime approaching with helpless despair. But she was determined to break this cycle of determination, which always ended in her own violent anger and Caroline's rebellious screams.

With an effort of will which exhausted her, she learned to put Caroline's food in front of her, and then go out of the room altogether. When she came back, she forbade herself to notice the unpleasant fly-covered mess on the high chair. She quickly lifted the child out, and washed her, and set her back in her pen without saying a word. Day after day, Martha lay face down on the bed, at every meal-time, her fingers stuck in her ears, reading, while Caroline yelled for attention next door. Slowly the yells lessened. There came a point where the child received her food and ate it. Martha returned from her exile in the bedroom, the victory won. She had succeeded in defeating the demon of antagonism.

And now she was able to cook the food and serve Caroline with it and not care if she ate it or not. And of course, now it was eaten. And Martha existed on hastily cut slabs of bread and butter and tea. She could not be interested in food unless she was cooking it for someone with whom she would share it afterwards. Women living by themselves can starve themselves into a sickness without knowing what is wrong with them.

Then she became perversely sad because she had won the victory. It seemed that something must have snapped between her and her daughter. It increased that persistent uneasiness, which expressed itself in those interminable puzzled humorous monologues: 'It's all very well, Caroline, but there must be something wrong when you have to learn *not* to care ... because the trouble with me is not that I care too much, but that I care too little—you'd be relieved, my poor brat, if you knew that when you were with my mother, I never thought of you at all—that's a guarantee of your future emotional safety, isn't it?

Silence, while Caroline pursued her own interests about the room; if the silence persisted, however, she cocked a bright enquiring eye towards her mother. 'But what I can't understand is this. Two years ago, I was as free as air. I could have done anything, been anything. Because the essence of the day-dreams of every girl who isn't married is just that: it's the one time they are more free than men. Men *have* to be something, but you'll find when you grow up my poor child that you'll see yourself as a ballet dancer, or business executive, or the wife of a Prime Minister, or the mistress of somebody important, or even in extreme moments a nun or a missionary. You'll imagine yourself doing all sorts of things in all sorts of countries; but the point is, your will will be your limit. Anything'll be possible. But you will not see yourself sitting in a small room bound for twenty-four hours of day with years of it in front of you to a small child. For God's sake, Caroline, don't marry young, I'll stop you marrying young if I have to lock you up. But I can't do that,' concluded Martha humorously, 'because that would be putting pressure on you, and that's the unforgivable sin. All I can promise is that I won't put any pressure on you of any kind. I simply *won't care* ... But supposing that not caring is only the most subtle and deadly way of putting pressure on people —what then? ... but what is most difficult is this. If you read novels and diaries, women didn't seem to have these problems—is it quite different in the space of about fifty years? Or do you suppose they didn't tell the truth, the novelists? In the books, the young and idealistic girls gets married, has a baby—she at once turns into something quite different; and she is perfectly happy to spend her whole life bringing up children with a tedious husband. Natasha for instance ... she was content to be an old hen, fussing and dull ... but supposing all the time she saw a picture of herself as she had been, and saw herself as what she had become and was miserable? What then? Because either that's the truth, or there is a completely new kind of woman in the world, and surely that isn't possible, what do you think, Caroline?'

All the morning, sunlight moved and deployed around the flat. After lunch the sun had moved away; the rooms were warm, airless, stagnant. And then Martha put Caroline into her push-chair, and filled in the time by wheeling her around the streets for an hour, two hours, three hours. Or she sat in a park under a tree with dozens of other young mothers and nannies, watching the children play. This period of the day seemed to concentrate into it the essence of boredom. It was boredom like an illness. But at six in the evening, Caroline was washed, fed, and put into her cot. Silence descended. Martha was free. She could go out, see people, go to the pictures. But she did not. She sat alone, reading and thinking interminably, turning over and over in her mind this guilty weight of thoughts, which were always the same. Those people who have been brought up in the non-conformist pattern may shed God, turn the principles they were brought up in upside down; but they may always be relied upon to torment themselves satisfactorily with problems of right behaviour. From these dreary self-searchings there emerged a definite idea: that there must be if not in literature, which evaded these problems, then in life, that woman who combined a warm accepting femininity and motherhood with being what Martha described vaguely but to her own satisfaction as 'a person'. She must look for her. Then one day she saw Stella in the street. They exchanged those gay guilty promises to come and see each other which people do who are dropping out of each other's lives. Afterwards Martha thought that Stella looked very contented. She had changed. Two years ago she had been a lithe alive beautiful young woman. Having a baby had turned her into a stout and handsome matron, very smart, competent and—this was the point, happy. Or so it seemed in retrospect. Thinking wistfully for several days about Stella's unfailing self-assurance in whatever role life asked her to play, turned her, for Martha, into a symbol of satisfactory womanhood. On an impulse then, she dropped Caroline in the house across the park with her mother, and drove out to the house in the suburbs where Stella now lived with her mother.

37 A Man Infatuated—and Out of Love

From *Liber Amoris*

by William Hazlitt

William Hazlitt (1778–1830) was a writer on art and drama and an essayist and literary critic. He was a friend of most of the poets and writers of the day. The Liber Amoris, *1823, is the record of a miserable infatution he had for his landlady's daughter.*

There is an excellent introduction by Charles Morgan to the Liber Amoris *in the edition published by Peter Nevill in 1948. It discusses both the psychology of Hazlitt and the psychology of 'falling in love' and is interesting about why this was a condemned and forbidden book to the Victorians.*

Unaltered Love. Shall I not love her for herself alone, in spite of fickleness and folly? To love her for her regard to me, is not to love her, but myself. She has robbed me of herself; shall she also rob me of my love of her? Did I not live on her smile? Is it less sweet because it is withdrawn from me? Did I not adore her every grace? Does she bend less enchantingly, because she has turned from me to another? Is my love then in the power of fortune, or of her caprice? No, I will have it lasting as it is pure; and I will make a Goddess of her, and build a temple to her in my heart, and worship her on indestructible altars, and raise statues to her: and my homage shall be unblemished as her unrivalled symmetry of form; and when that fails, the memory of it shall survive; and my bosom shall be proof to scorn, as hers has been to pity; and I will pursue her with an unrelenting love, and sue to be her slave, and tend her steps without notice and without reward; and serve her living, and mourn for her when dead. And thus my love will have shewn itself superior to her hate; and I shall triumph and then die. This is my idea of the only true and heroic love! Such is mine for her.

* * *

I did not sleep a wink all that night; nor did I know till the next day the full meaning of what had happened to me. With the morning's light, conviction glared in upon me that I had not only lost her for ever—but every feeling I had ever had towards her—respect, tenderness, pity—all but my fatal passion, was gone. The whole was a mockery, a frightful illusion. I had embraced the false Florimel instead of the true; or was like the man in the *Arabian Nights* who had married a *goul*. How different was the idea I once had of her! Was this she,

> Who had been beguiled—she who was made
> Within a gentle bosom to be laid—
> To bless and to be blessed—to be heart-bare
> To one who found his bettered likeness there—
> To think for ever with him, like a bride—
> To haunt his eye, like taste personified—
> To double his delight, to share his sorrow,
> And like a morning beam, wake to him every morrow?

I saw her pale, cold form glide silent by me, dead to shame as to pity. Still I seemed to clasp this piece of witchcraft to my bosom; this lifeless image, which was all that was left of my love, was the only thing to which my sad heart clung. Were she dead, should I not wish to gaze once more upon her pallid features? She is dead to me; but what she once was to me can never die! The agony, the conflict of hope and fear, of adoration and jealousy is over; or it would, ere long, have ended with my life. I am no more lifted now to Heaven, and then plunged in the abyss; but I seem to have been thrown from the top of a precipice, and to lie grovelling, stunned, and stupified. I am melancholy, lonesome, and weaker than a child. The worst is, I have no prospect of any alteration for the better: she has cut off all possibility of a reconcilement at any future period. Were she even to return to her former pretended fondness and endearments, I could have no pleasure, no confidence in them. I can scarce make out the contradiction to myself.

I strive to think she always was what I now know she is; but I have great difficulty in it, and can hardly believe but that she still *is* what she so long *seemed*. Poor thing! I am afraid she is little better off herself; nor do I see what is to become of her, unless she throws off the mask at once and runs a-mock at infamy. She is exposed and laid bare to all those whose opinion she set a value upon. Yet she held her head very high, and must feel (if she feels anything) proportionably mortified—A more complete experiment on character was never made. If I had not met her lover immediately after I parted with her, it would have been nothing. I might have supposed she had changed her mind in my absence, and had given him the preference as soon as she felt it, and even shewn her delicacy in declining any further intimacy with me. But it comes out that she had gone on in the most forward and familiar way with both at once—(she could not change her mind in passing from one room to another)—told both the same bare-faced and unblushing falsehoods, like the commonest creature; received presents from me to the very last, and wished to keep up the game still longer, either to gratify her humour, her avarice, or her vanity, in playing with my passion, or have me as a *dernier resort* in case of accidents. Again, it would have been nothing, if she had not come up with her demure, well-composed, wheedling looks that morning, and then met me in the evening in a situation which (she believed) might kill me on the spot, with no more feeling than a common courtesan shews, who *bilks* a customer, and passes him, leering up at her bully, the moment after. If there had been the frailty of passion, it would have been excusable; but she is a practised, callous, jilt, a regular lodging-house decoy, played off by her mother upon the lodgers, one after another, applying them to her different purpose, laughing at them in turns, and herself the probable dupe and victim of some favourite gallant in the end. I know all this; but what do I gain by it, unless I could find some one with her shape and air, to supply the place of that lovely apparition...

...One more count finishes the indictment. She not only discovered the most hardened indifference to the feelings of others; she has not shewn the least regard to her own character, or shame when she was detected. When found out, she seemed to say 'Well, what if I am? I have played the game as long as I could; and if I could keep it up no longer, it was not for want of good will.' Her colouring once or twice is the only sign of grace she has exhibited. Such is the creature on whom I had thrown away my heart and soul—one who was incapable of feeling the commonest emotions of human nature, as they regarded herself or anyone else. 'She had no feelings with respect to herself' she often said. She, in fact, knows what she is, and recoils from the good opinion or sympathy of others which she feels to be founded on a deception, so that my overweening opinion of her must have appeared like irony or direct insult. My seeing her in the street has gone a good way to satisfy me. Her manner there explains her manner in-doors to be conscious and overdone; and besides she looks but indifferently. She is diminutive in stature, and her measured step and timid air do not suit these public airings. I am afraid she will soon grow common to my imagination, as well as worthless in herself. Her image seems 'fast going in the wastes of time', like a need that the wave bears farther and farther from me. Alas! thou poor hapless need, when I entirely lose sight of thee, and for ever, no flower will ever bloom on earth to glad my heart again.

38 Being a Mother

From *Look the Other Way*

by John Branfield

John Branfield was born in 1930 and is the author of three novels: A Flag in the Map, *1960,* Look the Other Way, *1963, and* In the Country, *1966. He is married with three children.* Look the Other Way *is a witty and detailed account of modern living and loving in a household full of children.*

Charles was getting ready to cut the meat. This was one of his jobs, not because it belonged by tradition to the head of the family, but simply because Patricia made such a mess of it. He took the carving knife and made some pretence of sharpening it, knocking it up and down against the steel and probably making it blunter. Then he sliced away at their lump of pork. They always had their roast hot on Saturdays, cold on Sundays. It was nearly all fat, they usually got the cheapest made-up joints that Dewhursts sold. He picked out some of the lean and chopped it up small for the children.

Pat put on the soup and went to fetch the baby from upstairs. In the breakfast-room the girls sat at the table, waiting. Charles had got it all ready. Paul wanted to sit up too, so she lifted him into his high-chair. They had all their meals in the breakfast-room, as Charles called it; she thought it was the kitchen really, and the kitchen was the scullery. What should have been the dining-room was the playroom.

When she came back she noticed that Judith had drunk all her water, and out of the corner of her eye she saw her turning her glass upside-down. 'Look, Alison,' she said.

Immediately Alison did the same, forgetting that her glass was still full. She gazed in horror at the water spreading over the table, and then dripping over the edge into the lap of her dungarees; she began to whimper.

'Naughty girl,' said Judith.

Charles, coming in with their plates, saw her holding the upturned glass. 'You did that deliberately,' he said. 'I saw you.'

'Give her a smack, Daddy.'

'Yes, but you didn't see what Judy did,' said Pat. 'She started it.'

She dumped the baby in his pram—he was no trouble at all, thank goodness; they got easier every time—and fetched a dish-cloth to mop up the water. 'Why is it always such a zoo at mealtimes?' she complained. She took everything off the table and put on a clean cloth. 'Now that's the last one I've got, so don't upset anything else on it.'

They began banging their spoons on their plates as they waited for their dinner. Charles put his hands to his ears, and looked imploringly at Patricia, who was feeding the baby in his pram in the kitchen, her mouth opening and closing with his, and who was trying to do the toast at the same time. She caught sight of Charles's pained expression.

'You do something about them,' she said.

'Hush,' said Charles, who would rather deal with a class of thirty-five fifteen-year-olds than three under-fives.

'If I've got to come up there you'll know it,' called Pat.

The banging faltered for a moment, then recovered. Pat was preparing herself for a pitched battle when the breakfast-room door opened and Mathewson came in holding a large cardboard box in front of him. The noise stopped.

'I'm sorry, I knocked but I don't think anyone heard me.'

'I'm not surprised.'

'What's this, the town band?'

'Yes,' shouted the girls. 'We're soldiers,' shouted Alison. And they began to bang their plates again.

'Oh dear, I said the wrong thing there,' said Mathewson. 'Listen, I can make a noise.'

He shook his cardboard box, and a lot of bottles chinked together.

'Here's Humpty Dumpty, in Afro-Cuban style.' He shook out the rhythm; the fall was impressive. He was staggering a bit towards the end, the bottles were heavy to hold out and shake around.

'What's in that box, Mr. Man?'

'What's in the box, Mr. Man?' echoed the younger one.

'Don't be rude,' said Pat.

'Little more than empties, I almost threw them out before coming here. But there's a drop in the bottom of most of them, if you'd like a drink before lunch?'

'Can we have a look?' asked Patricia. She went down on her knees beside the box, and drew out one bottle after the other, giving exclamations of recognition and delight. The two girls got down and joined in, pulling out bottles and holding them up. It was like Christmas again.

'What will you have?'

'I don't know, there's so many.'

'Let's put back the unsuitable ones, then you'll be able to see.' He picked up the brandy, the Cointreau, a bottle of whisky.

'In France they drink whisky as an aperitif,' said Charles.

'That's just the sort of damn fool thing they would do,' said Henry.

'It's smart, simply because it's so dear,' muttered Charles, who was slightly taken aback by Henry's vehemence. 'It's snobbish really.'

'*Le snobisme*,' said Henry, giving it a lot of feeling and relishing a highly exaggerated pronunciation. 'Here's a pretty one, Judith, *crème de menthe*.' Again the exaggerated French accent, obviously for Charles's benefit.

'They're like skittles,' said Judy.

'Now Mummy,' said Henry. 'Let me mix you a Martini. Two to one?'

'Half and half,' said Pat. 'Wait a minute, I'd better wash the glasses. They've probably got spiders' web in them.' She rushed back to the kitchen.

'France would be all right,' she heard Henry saying, 'if it weren't for the French.'

When she returned he poured two Martinis, and Charles had a Noilly Prat, which gave Henry some more fun with his accent, first of all pretending that he didn't know any French and making it sound like an English footballer, and then doing it as though he was in a class practising French vowel sounds.

The girls clamoured for a drink.

'What do you think, Daddy?'

'Just a tiny sip, no more.'

'The voice of authority,' murmured Henry.

'He's a real Victorian father, is Charles.'

'He lays down the law, does he?'

Charles ignored their remarks. 'Don't you like the French then?' he asked.

'I detest them,' said Henry cheerfully.

'It's like medicine,' said Alison, meaning that she liked it.

'Will I go rolling home now?' asked Judy.

'You would if you drank a lot.'

'How would I go if I went rolling home?'

'You know, dear.'

'I don't know, Mummy.'

'Daddy'll show you.'

'Well, you just . . . roll,' said Charles. 'Only silly people do it.'

'Like this,' said Henry, and he rolled to the door and back. He didn't overdo it, he was like one of those wooden toy men with a weight in the bottom, who sway from side to side but always bob upright again. When he turned back he had put on a bleary, lugubrious expression.

The performance was quite extraordinarily successfully. The two girls practically had hysterics, they had clearly never seen anything so funny before.

'It seems rather an extreme opinion to detest them all,' said Charles, but no one heard him. The girls were shouting for more.

So he did it again.

'You're Mr. Winebottle,' shouted Judith.

'Oh, I'm Mr. Winebottle, am I?'

'You're Mr. Winebottle,' echoed Alison.

'Then you're Miss Corkscrew.'

This sally was greeted with further shrieks of laughter.

'You're Mr. Running Nose.'

'Him Big Chief Running Nose.' He looked apologetically at Charles.

'I'm afraid my repartee isn't exactly scintillating.'

'You're Mr. Smelly Pyjamas.'

'That'll do,' said Patricia. 'It's time everyone sat down, or they'll be too excited to eat.'

'Mademoiselle Ju-dith,' said Henry, drawing out her chair for her. He looked puzzled, because this name produced no hilarious reaction.

'Charles wanted to give them French names,' said Patricia, 'but I put my foot down.'

'Thank goodness for that,' said Henry, as though genuinely relieved. He tried out their names with a French pronunciation, ending with Madame Pa-treesha, which he said he liked the sound of, and Charles said it had a certain snobbish value too, it was the sort of name a model might give herself. Pat asked which sort of model, the ones that advertise all positions undertaken, and Charles said no, of course not, he meant a fashion model.

Madame Pa-treesha brought in the toast and bowls of soup. Each time she came in Henry got to his feet—'No, do sit down please'—and thereafter he made a sort of gesture of rising, lifting his behind a few inches off the chair. Charles was shamed into doing the same, and this pantomime went on until she eventually sat down.

'Ah, melba toast,' exclaimed Henry. 'I do like melba toast.'

'I thought it was just ordinary toast,' said Pat.

'I hate these flaccid rolls they give you nowadays—.'

'Judy, you're wriggling,' exclaimed Pat.

'No, I'm not wriggling.'

'You didn't go before dinner, did you?'

'I did.'

'You didn't.'

'I DID.'

'What do you think, Daddy?'

'If she says she did, we must believe her.'

'All right. But if you're wet you won't have any sweets after dinner.'

Judith thought about it. 'Perhaps I'd better go, to make sure.'

She got down from the table.

'You can't dislike them all,' said Charles. 'It's a very sweeping statement. I should be interested to know—'

'What's the matter with that little girl?' said Pat.

They all looked at Alison. She was weeping quietly into her soup.

'Darling, what is it?'

'I want a proper dinner,' she sobbed.

'But you have your soup first, then you have your proper dinner.'

She began crying aloud. 'I want my dummy-dum.'

'Go and get it then, under your pillow.'

She got down from the table.

'A moment's peace,' sighed Patricia. 'Yes, now what was it you were saying, Charles?'

But then Judith was back. 'I've been rather a silly girl,' she said, and laughed nervously. 'I didn't pull my pants down very well and I got them a tiny bit wet—not very much.'

'You were wet before, weren't you?'

'No, I wasn't.'

'It was all that water you drank. Well, we won't make a fuss about it now.'

'I can have my sweets, can't I?'

'Eat up your soup.' She turned to Henry. 'Mr. Mathewson, another piece of toast—what did you call it?'

'Melba toast, after the singer, I suppose.'

'I thought that was peaches.'

'I should like to know your reasons.'

'My sweets after dinner.'

'Judy, I'm talking to Mr. Mathewson.'

'Mummy, I can't generalise.'

'Dummy-dums.'

'Individuals.'

'Toast too.'

No one was really communicating.

'BE QUIARK EVERYONE,' shouted Judith, 'I truly am talking to you.'

They were quiet, except for Paul who broke wind.

Judith turned on him. 'And you too, or I'll smack your bott'n.'

There was complete silence.

'Now Judy, what do you want to say?' asked Pat.

'What a little martinet,' said Henry. 'I wish my discipline was half as good.'

But Judy went coy, and wouldn't say it. She got down and whispered to her Mummy.

'No, not that, dear. Say "Uncle Henry".'

'I'm not very fond of the uncle, just say Henry.'

'She wants to know if Henry has a car.'

'Like all the young ladies! Yes, I have a car.'

'Will you take us for a ride?'

'Judith!' exclaimed Patricia and Charles simultaneously.

'I'd like to take you for a ride.'

'One day perhaps, not today,' said Pat.

'I won't have her asking people for things,' said Charles.

'Now let me have all your bowls,' said Pat. 'I've got to wash them or we won't have anything to put our pudding in.'

'Thank you,' said Henry, handing up his bowl. 'That was most delicious.'

'Thank Mr. Heinz.'

'Then it must be the way you warmed it up.'

'It's always nicer if you haven't had to do it yourself. You'll have to come down and join us regularly.'

She carried the dishes out to the kitchen and Charles followed her. She thought he was going to say something about her spontaneous invitation, but he went to the cupboard under the sink and took out a bottle of wine.

'I thought it was for Robert tomorrow night,' she said.

'I'll have to get another.'

Although Charles was never very keen on having visitors, when they were once there he quite liked to play the part of host. He was only mean in anticipation. She heard him saying as he returned to the breakfast-room to draw the cork, 'I'm sorry, it should have been *débouché* a couple of hours ago.' And then Henry asking what it was, and saying, 'Hm. Mâcon '57; that should be very good,' in a very knowledgeable sort of way. She smiled to herself; it amused her, the way they were so serious and worldly.

So when she came back she said, 'If it's not warm enough, stick it on the stove for a while.'

Charles was outraged. 'Stick it on the stove!' he repeated.

'You'd ruin it, it's sacrilege.'

But Henry only laughed; he seemed to realise that she was teasing him.

Charles poured the wine. She liked to watch him perform this ritual, it was Charles at his most Charles-ish. He began with the traditional drop in his own glass, intended to remove the oil with which wine was once sealed but which, of course, was no longer there. If you didn't know, you would have thought that he had started to serve himself, then suddenly remembered his manners and gone on to someone else. But if you know, you knew it was a custom that went back hundreds of years.

He half-filled Patricia's tumbler, then gave the bottle a twist and raised it with a flourish; not a drop dripped on to the cloth. He paused with the neck over Henry's glass.

'You do drink French wine, do you?'

'Of course I do, I like all the products of France. It's only the people I can't stand.'

'Why?'

'I like Italians though, they're quite different. They welcome you, in three minutes you feel you've been one of the family all your life.'

'I don't know that I want to feel one of the family,' said Charles.

'All right then, go to the other extreme. Take a people like the Dutch. Sturdy, solid, reserved—I can understand anyone liking them. But the French!'

Pat had never liked the French much, but if she said so to Charles he tried to squash her with a lecture about *la douce France* and its contribution, historical, philosophical and cultural, to European civilisation. She was surprised, then, when he said no more to Henry, but busied himself colouring the girls' water with wine. When he had finished, both men raised their glasses and circled them round beneath their noses.

Henry gave an appreciative sigh. 'It reminds me rather of the '47,' he said slowly and reflectively, in a parody of a clubman's voice. 'What a year, by Jove!' He arched his rather fine nostrils and lifted his straight nose critically into the air. 'But of course, it hasn't quite the bouquet of the '55, do you think?'

'What can you expect for 7s. 6d.?' said Pat.

'It's a decent *vin ordinaire*,' said Charles.

'Very decent,' said Henry, to show that he wasn't really at all critical. 'And Patreesha, my favourite potatoes! How did you know?'

'I'm sorry they aren't sauté.'

'But I love creamed potatoes.'

'Charles only likes them sauté, but they're dreadful at the moment, they fall to pieces.'

'Charles is spoilt I can see.'

With one finger over the hole, Charles was pretending to sprinkle salt over the children's mash. Henry discovered the apple sauce; that was a favourite too. There was only the meat left, and he couldn't very well exclaim about that, thought Pat. But he did; he liked pork, more than any other meat. Perhaps so, she thought, but it didn't necessarily mean this pork.

He was reminded of a time in Italy, when he had lunch with an Italian family. 'They were desperately poor, six of them living in one room, the plaster falling off the ceiling—'

'Just like us,' said Pat. She glanced up. The plaster wasn't actually falling off, but the boiler stove had turned it grey in places. Charles had better do it in the Easter holidays.

'Not at all,' said Henry, 'except in the warmth of their welcome.' He went on with his story.

We've done nothing special, though Pat. She didn't feel that they were at all Italian, not a bit like these people that Henry was describing, with their spontaneity, their quickness, their vivacity.

With her head down she shovelled away her food. The speed at which she ate increased with each child. It had to,

137

she had to grab what she could quickly, between running in and out and attending to the children. She suddenly realised that her plate was almost empty, while Henry's was hardly touched. He was talking so much, and illustrating what he had to say with such large Italianate gestures, that he had had time to eat no more than two or three mouthfuls of his favourite pork, favourite apple sauce and favourite creamed potatoes. She abruptly slowed down her pace, and toyed with the remaining forkfuls.

Alison had got no further with her dinner than Henry. She pushed it aside, knocking it into Judith's plate. Judith promptly pushed it back, and they began a sort of see-saw with the plate of dinner in the middle. Both complained loudly about the other.

'NO PUDDINGS for any little girl who doesn't eat up ALL HER DINNER,' shouted Patricia. 'I'm sorry, Henry. Please go on.'

'I'll have some pudding, won't I, Mummy?' said Judith, who had nearly finished. 'And Alison won't have nenny.'

'Ess,' said Alison.

'Then both of you be quiet and eat up your dinner.'

Henry now saw how little he had eaten, and began to make up for lost time. He folded half of the meat on to his fork at once, and ate it in one mouthful.

Patricia put her hand on his arm. 'Take your time,' she said. 'We all gobble.'

He shook his head, chewed seriously, waited until he had cleared his mouth, and then said, 'But I don't want to miss any puddings.'

'There girls, look at Uncle Henry. He doesn't talk with his mouth full. I wish I could get you to do that. And he's eating up ALL HIS DINNER.'

'Good boy,' said Judy.

'Ess,' said Alison.

Henry made a good-little-boy face, with lips pursed together in a prim smile and eyes looking up to heaven.

'That suits you,' said Pat. 'I bet you were a horribly good little boy.'

'As a matter of fact, I was very wicked.'

'Eat up your dinner,' whispered Judith urgently. 'Or you won't have nenny pudding.'

'Oh dear, yes; I won't say another word.'

'Make that funny face again.'

So he ate the rest of his dinner with the angelic, butter-wouldn't-melt-in-his-mouth look on his face, and the girls watched him and giggled, and Pat managed to get a few spoonfuls of dinner into Alison, who didn't ralise she was eating them. She fetched the dishes that she had washed.

'Whose turn is it for the bunny rabbits?' she asked.

'Mine,' shouted Judith.'

'Mine,' shouted Alison.

Each dish was different, though each had once belonged to a set.

There was a Bunnykins, a Sooty-in-his-washtub, a blue pyrex, a plain white, a dirty brown, bought in a sale and reduced because of the colour, and a red plastic picnic dish.

'Who had it for soup?'

'Paul.'

'Who had it for breakfast then?'

'I had it at breakfast,' said Judith earnestly, 'because Alison didn't want any corncakes. Only, she had it for dinner yesterday, and it's my turn today.'

'Look, Alison,' said Pat, as though she had just found something wonderful. 'Who would like a lovely birdie blue dish that you can see through?'

'I', said Alison doubtfully.

'That's good girl.'

'I want a birdie blue one too,' said Judy.

'YOU'LL BOTH HAVE WHAT YOU'VE GOT. We ought to let our guest choose first. Which would you like, guest?'

'You can have the bunny rabbits if you like,' said Judith.

'No, thank you. They're both lovely dishes, but I'll have Sooty-in-the-washtub, if I may.'

Patricia fetched the pudding; rice with a coffee meringue top. The children drew in their breath appreciatively, and began banging their spoons. They were itching to have a go at the pudding itself, tempted by its crispness.

'Don't bang the meringue,' she warned. 'It's their

favourite pudding,' she said to Henry, and then added, 'I suppose it's your favourite pudding, too?'

'How did you guess?' said Henry. 'Though as a matter of fact it's not my most favourite pudding at all.'

'Would you rather have some fruit?'

'Oh no, I'm not going to miss the rice.'

'Do you usually eat it?'

'It's usually too much bother to prepare, just for one.'

'But do you like it?'

'Yes, I've got quite a thing about rice.'

'A thing for or against.'

Henry gave up trying to sound enthusiastic. 'Against,' he admitted, in a small voice.

'Then why don't you say so? It's much better to come straight out with it. If I hadn't found out I might have gone on making rice puddings every time you came, thinking you liked them. And I bet you would have eaten them too, and pretended they were delicious.'

'I'm afraid so.'

'What do you like?'

'All the wrong things, like boiled puddings.'

'I'll make you one next time.'

'And could I have a little rice now? A mere *soupçon*.'

The word lent itself to his exaggerated French accent, he thrust his lips forward on the first syllable, and almost swallowed them on the second. 'Which reminds me of a story—tell me if you've heard it before—about a maiden lady who had never wanted to give her friends any trouble, so she went to an undertaker to make arrangements for her own funeral. She chose a coffin, and the undertaker explained that for spinsters it was usual to have a white lining, and for married women a purple lining. "Oh well, in that case," she said, "I'll have white with the merest trimming of purple".'

'What are you laughing about?' asked Judy suspiciously.

'I think perhaps they've had too much wine to drink,' said Charles, who didn't laugh easily.

'They're very silly people.'

Alison wasn't listening to them, she was too busy eating

her pudding. She ate with her eyes screwed up tight, and a sort of purring noise came from her.

'She's enjoying it,' said Pat. 'Is Daddy enjoying his?'

Charles didn't like rice any more than Henry, and he too had only had a mere symbol.

'All stop and listen to Daddy enjoying his rice pudding.'

Obediently he took a spoonful. He cut through the crust of the meringue; the inside was greenish-brown, like the inside of a puff-ball. He put it in his mouth.

'Mmmmm . . .' he went.'

'That's not very loud, is it?'

'MMMMM . . .'

'That's better. And now Henry.'

He needed no second bidding. He was humming away at the top of his voice, and his face was set in an agony of ecstasy.

'More,' shouted Alison, pushing up her plate. 'I want more. Because I like it, that's why. I want that bit and that bit and that bit. . . .' And she jabbed her spoon at every part of the dish.

She began showing off, as she waited for her next helping. She counted inaccurately up to ten. She went through the days of the week: 'Monday, Tuesday, Wednesday, Yesterday.'

She started shaking her head rapidly from side to side, and Paul in his high-chair copied her. The movement seemed to hypnotise them, they took no notice of orders to stop but went on faster and faster. It made Pat feel ill, to think of the waves on their semi-circular canals.

She only stopped when a second helping was put in front of her. Charles and Henry went on to the cheese, with which they finished the rest of the wine. Henry started off on his Italian story again about how they had managed to beg, borrow or steal an old car after lunch, and they had all piled in and gone off to some local beauty spot. But he didn't get far, because from that point the meal rapidly disintegrated into chaos. The baby, tired of being left so long on his own, was howling in the kitchen. Paul tried to attract attention by setting a dishful of rice pudding upside down on his head. The girls sharpened their wits on Henry.

'I'm going to call you Mr. Jump-in-the-cupboard.'

'I'm going to put you in the dustbin.'

'I'm going to throw you down the chimney.'

For a while they elaborated their threats. Then they both stood on their chairs and shouted at the top of their voices, 'Marmalade pop.'

'Enough,' said Patricia. 'Into the playroom all of you.' She dragged Paul out of his chair, wiped him over, and sent them all packing. She picked up baby David and sat him on her lap.

You could feel the silence settling down around them.

'Cigarette?' asked Henry quietly.

She glanced at Charles.

'Go on, you don't have to ask your husband, do you?'

'Charles doesn't like to see a woman smoking when she's holding a baby.'

So Charles reached across and took David from her.

Henry flicked his lighter, and she inclined her face towards the flame. She leaned back, and surveyed the scene through a cloud of cigarette smoke.

'It's like a battlefield,' she sighed. The table was in a dreadful mess, and on the floor were dollops of mashed potato and rice pudding.

'You'll have to have a meal with us in the evening next time, when the children are out of the way.'

'But I enjoy them.'

'In small doses, that's enough for most people.'

'They're wonderful.'

'They could have been worse, I suppose.'

Henry smiled reflectively. 'I can't remember when I last enjoyed a meal so much.'

'But we couldn't say a thing.' She really couldn't understand why it should have been so enjoyable. The children had behaved pretty badly.

'I'll make you your coffee,' she said. 'I can get the washing-up done while you're drinking it.'

But Henry leapt to his feet. 'I'll help to wash up,' he said. 'It's the least I can do.'

39 A Man in Two Minds

From *Nightmare Abbey*

by Thomas Love Peacock

*Thomas Love Peacock (1785–1866) was a novelist and poet and is best known for his satires—*Headlong Hall, *1816,* Nightmare Abbey, *1818,* Crotchet Castle, *1831, and* Gryll Grange, *1860. He collects a party of odd characters in a country house and lets them converse. Most of the well-known figures of the day are caricatured. Peacock was a great friend of Shelley who appears as Scythrop in* Nightmare Abbey. *Byron and Coleridge also appear as Mr. Cypress and Mr. Flosky.*

Scythrop did not dare to mention the name of Marionetta; he trembled lest some unlucky accident should reveal it to Stella, though he scarcely knew what result to wish or anticipate, and lived in the double fever of a perpetual dilemma. He could not dissemble to himself that he was in love, at the same time, with two damsels of minds and habits as remote as the antipodes. The scale of predilection always inclined to the fair one who happened to be present; but the absent was never effectually outweighed, though the degress of exaltation and depression varied according to accidental variations in the outward and visible signs of the inward and spiritual graces of his respective charmers. Passing and repassing several times a day from the company of the one to that of the other, he was like a shuttlecock between two battledores, changing its direction as rapidly as the oscillations of a pendulum, receiving many a hard knock on the core of a sensitive heart, and flying from point to point on the feathers of a super-sublimated head. This was an awful state of things. He had as now as much mystery about him as any romantic transcendentalist or transcendental romancer could desire. He had his esoterical and his exoterical love. He could not endure the thought of losing either of them, but he trembled when he imagined the possibility that some fatal discovery might deprive him of both. The old proverbs concerning two strings to a bow gave him some gleams of comfort; but that concerning two stools occurred to him more frequently, and covered his forehead with a cold perspiration. With Stella, he could indulge freely in all his romantic and philosophical visions. He could build castles in the air, and she would pile towers and turrets on his imaginary edifices. With Marionetta it was otherwise: she knew nothing of the world and society beyond the sphere of her own experience. Her life was all music and sunshine, and she wondered what any one could see to complain of in such a pleasant state of things. She loved Scythrop, she hardly knew why; indeed she was not always sure that she loved him at all: she felt her fondness increase or diminish in an inverse ratio to his. When she had manoeuvred him into a fever of passionate love, she often felt and always assumed indifference: if she found that her coldness was contagious, and that Scythrop either was, or pretended to be, as indifferent as herself, she would become doubly kind, and raise him again to that elevation from which she had previously thrown him down. Thus, when his love was flowing, hers was ebbing: when his was ebbing, hers was flowing. Now and then there were moments of level tide, when reciprocal affection seemed to promise imperturbable harmony; but Scythrop could scarcely resign his spirit to the pleasing illusion, before the pinnace of the lover's affections was caught in some eddy of the lady's caprice, and he was whirled away from the shore of his hopes, without rudder or compass, into an ocean of mists and storms. It resulted from this system of conduct, that all that passed between Scythrop and Marionetta consisted in making and unmaking love. He had no opportunity to take measure of her understanding by conversations on general subjects, and on his favourite designs; and, being left in this respect to the exercise of indefinite conjecture, he took it for granted, as most lovers would do in similar circumstances, that she had great natural talents, which she wasted at present on trifles: but coquetry would end with marriage, and leave room for philosophy to exert its influence on her mind. Stella had no coquetry, no disguise: she was an enthusiast in subjects of general interest, and her conduct to Scythrop was always uniform, or rather showed a regular profession of partiality which seemed fast ripening into love.

40 If Shakespeare Had Been a Woman

From *A Room of One's Own*

by Virginia Woolf

For notes on Virginia Woolf see Extract No. 2 The Waves. *A* Room of One's Own *is required reading for any girl who wishes to become a writer.*

Let me imagine, since facts are so hard to come by, what would have happened had Shakespeare had a wonderfully gifted sister, called Judith, let us say. Shakespeare himself went, very probably—his mother was an heiress—to the grammar school, where he may have learnt Latin—Ovid, Virgil and Horace—and the elements of grammar and logic. He was, it is well known, a wild boy who poached rabbits, perhaps shot a deer, and had, rather sooner than he should have done, to marry a woman in the neighbourhood, who bore him a child rather quicker than was right. That escapade sent him to seek his fortune in London. He had, it seemed, a taste for the theatre; he began by holding horses at the stage door. Very soon he got work in the theatre, became a successful actor, and lived at the hub of the universe, meeting everybody, knowing everybody, practising his art on the boards, exercising his wits in the streets, and even getting access to the palace of the queen. Meanwhile his extraordinarily gifted sister, let us suppose, remained at home. She was as adventurous, as imaginative, as agog to see the world as he was. But she was not sent to school. She had no chance of learning grammar and logic, let alone of reading Horace and Virgil. She picked up a book now and then, one of her brother's perhaps, and read a few pages. But then her parents came in and told her to mend the stockings or mind the stew and not moon about with books and papers. They would have spoken sharply but kindly, for they were substantial people who knew the conditions of life for a woman and loved their daughter —indeed, more likely than not she was the apple of her father's eye. Perhaps she scribbled some pages up in an apple loft on the sly, but was careful to hide them or set fire to them. Soon, however, before she was out of her teens, she was to be betrothed to the son of a neighbouring woolstapler. She cried out that marriage was hateful to her, and for that she was severely beaten by her father. Then he ceased to scold her. He begged her instead not to hurt him, not to shame him in this matter of her marriage. He would give her a chain of beads or a fine petticoat, he said; and there were tears in his eyes. How could she disobey him? How could she break his heart? The force of her own gift alone drove her to it. She made up a small parcel of her belongings, let herself down by a rope one summer's night and took the road to London. She was not seventeen. The birds that sang in the hedge were not more musical than she was. She had the quickest fancy, a gift like her brother's for the tune of words. Like him, she had a taste for the theatre. She stood at the stage door; she wanted to act, she said. Men laughed in her face. The manager—a fat, looselipped man—guffawed. He bellowed something about poodles dancing and women acting—no woman, he said, could possibly be an actress. He hinted—you can imagine what. She could get no training in her craft. Could she even seek her dinner in a tavern or roam the streets at midnight? Yet her genius was for fiction and lusted to feed abundantly upon the lives of men and women and the study of their ways. At last—for she was very young, oddly like Shakespeare the poet in her face, with the same grey eyes and rounded brows—at last Nick Greene the actor-manager took pity on her; she found herself with child by that gentleman and so—who shall measure the heat and violence of the poet's heart when caught and tangled in a woman's body?—killed herself one winter's night and lies buried at some cross-roads where the omnibuses now stop outside the Elephant and Castle.

That, more or less, is how the story would run, I think, if

a woman in Shakespeare's day had had Shakespeare's genius. But for my part it is unthinkable that any woman in Shakespeare's day should have had Shakespeare's genius. For genius like Shakespeare's is not born among labouring, uneducated, servile people.... How, then, could it have been born among women whose work began, according to Professor Trevelyan, almost before they were out of the nursery, who were forced to it by their parents and held to it by all the power of law and custom? Yet genius of a sort must have existed among women as it must have existed among the working classes. Now and again an Emily Brontë or a Robert Burns blazes out and proves its presence. But certainly it never got itself on to paper. When, however, one reads of a witch being ducked, of a woman possessed by devils, of a wise woman selling herbs, or even of a very remarkable man who had a mother, then I think we are on the track of a lost novelist, a suppressed poet, of some mute and inglorious Jane Austen, some Emily Brontë who dashed her brains out on the moor or mopped and mowed about the highways crazed with the torture that her gift had put her to. Indeed, I would venture to guess that Anon, who wrote so many poems without signing them, was often a woman. It was a woman Edward Fitzgerald, I think, suggested who made the ballads and the folk-songs, crooning them to her children, beguiling her spinning with them, or the length of the winter's night.

This may be true or it may be false—who can say?—but what is true in it, so it seemed to me, reviewing the story of Shakespeare's sister as I had made it, is that any woman born with a great gift in the sixteenth century would certainly have gone crazed, shot herself, or ended her days in some lonely cottage outside the village, half witch, half wizard, feared and mocked at. For it needs little skill in psychology to be sure that a highly gifted girl who had tried to use her gift for poetry would have been so thwarted and hindered by other people, so tortured and pulled asunder by her own contrary instincts, that she must have lost her health and sanity to a certainty. No girl could have walked to London and stood at a stage door and forced her way into the presence of actor-managers without doing herself a violence and suffering an anguish which may have been irrational—for chastity may be a fetish invented by certain societies for unknown reasons—but were none the less inevitable. Chastity had then, it has even now, a religious importance in a woman's life, and has so wrapped itself round with nerves and instincts that to cut it free and bring it to the light of day demands courage of the rarest. To have lived a free life in London in the sixteenth century would have meant for a women who was poet and playwright a nervous stress and dilemma which might well have killed her. Had she survived, whatever she had written would have been twisted and deformed, issuing from a strained and morbid imagination.

41 Being a Political Woman

From *The New Machiavelli*

by H. G. Wells

H. G. Wells (1866–1946) was the son of a small tradesman. After being apprenticed to a draper, he showed a thirst for knowledge and became a teacher and a graduate in science. After 1893 he became a full-time writer. His Experiment in Autobiography, *1934, is well worth reading and has just been re-published. He wrote* The History of Mr. Polly, Kipps, *many scientific romances which would now be called science fiction, e.g.* The Invisible Man *and* The Time Machine, *and many novels on social and political themes of which the best are* Love and Mr. Lewisham, Tono-Bungay, Ann Veronica *(on the suffragette movement) and* The New Machiavelli. *He also wrote histories of the world and books of popular science. He had enormous influence on the young intelligentsia of his day.*

I did for some time pick out Oscar Bailey, and then Esmeer showed him to me in elaborately confidential talk in a corner with a distinguished-looking stranger wearing a ribbon. Oscar had none of the fine appearance of his wife; he was a short sturdy figure with a rounded protruding abdomen and a curious broad, flattened, clean-shaven face that seemed nearly all forehead. He was of Anglo-Hungarian extraction, and I have always fancied something Mongolian in his type. He peered up with reddish swollen-looking eyes over gilt-edged glasses that were divided horizontally into portions of different refractive power, and he talked in an ingratiating undertone, with busy thin lips, and eager lisp and nervous movements of the hand.

People say that thirty years before at Oxford he was almost exactly the same eager, clever little man he was when I first met him. He had come up to Balliol bristling with extraordinary degrees and prizes captured in provincial and Irish and Scotch universities—and had made a name for himself as the most formidable dealer in exact fact the rhetoricians of the Union had ever had to encounter. From Oxford he had gone on to a position in the Higher Division of the Civil Service, I think in the War Office, and had speedily made a place for himself as a political journalist. He was a particularly neat controversialist, and very full of political and sociological ideas. He had a quite astounding memory for facts and a mastery of detailed analysis, and the time afforded scope for these gifts. The later eighties were full of politico-social discussion, and he became a prominent name upon the contents list of the *Nineteenth Century*, the *Fortnightly* and *Contemporary* chiefly as a half sympathetic but frequently very damaging critic of the socialism of that period. He won the immense respect of every one specially interest in social and political questions, he soon achieved the limited distinction that is awarded such capacity, and at that I think he would have remained for the rest of his life if he had not encountered Altiora.

But Altiora Macvitie was an altogether exceptional woman, an extraordinary mixture of qualities, the one woman in the world who could make something more out of Bailey than that. She had much of the vigour and handsomeness of a slender impudent young man, and an unscrupulousness altogether feminine. She was one of those women who are wanting in—what is the word?—muliebrity. She had courage and initiative and a philosophical way of handling questions. and she could be bored by regular work like a man. She was entirely unfitted for her sex's sphere. She was neither uncertain, coy nor hard to please, and altogether too stimulating and aggressive for any gentleman's hour of ease. Her cookery would have been about as sketchy as her handwriting, which was generally quite illegible, and she would have made, I feel sure, a shocking bad nurse. Yet you musn't imagine she was an inelegant or unbeautiful woman, and she is inconceivable to me in high collars or any sort of masculine garment. But her soul was bony, and at the base of her was a vanity gaunt and greedy! When she wasn't in a state of personal untidiness that was partly a protest against the waste of hours exacted by the toilet and partly a natural disinclination, she had a gypsy splendour of black and red and silver all her own. And somewhen in the early nineties she met and married Bailey.

I know very little about her early years. She was the only daughter of Sir Deighton Macvitie, who applied the iodoform process to cotton, and only his subsequent unfortunate attempts to become a Cotton King prevented her being a very rich woman. As it was she had a tolerable independence. She came into prominence as one of the more able of the little shoal of young women who were led into politico-philanthropic activities by the influence of the earlier novels of Mrs. Humphry Ward—the Marcella crop. She went 'slumming' with distinguished vigour, which was quite usual in those days—and returned from her experiences as an amateur flower girl with clear and original views about the problem—which is and always had been unusual. She had not married, I suppose because her standards were high, and men are cowards and with an instinctive appetite for muliebrity. She had kept house for her father by speaking occasionally to the housekeeper, butler and cook her mother had left her, and gathering the most interesting dinner parties she could, and had married off four orphan nieces in a harsh and successful manner. After her father's smash and death she came out as a writer upon social questions and a scathing critic of of the Charity Organisation Society, and she was three and thirty and a little at loose ends when she met Oscar Bailey, so to speak, in the *Contemporary Review*. The lurking woman in her nature was fascinated by the ease and precision with which the little man rolled over all sorts of important and authoritative people, she was the first to discover a sort of imaginative bigness in his still growing mind, the forehead perhaps carried him off physically, and she took occasion to meet and subjugate him, and, so soon as he had sufficiently recovered from his abject humility and a certain panic at her attentions, marry him.

This had opened a new phase in the lives of Bailey and herself. The two supplemented each other to an extraordinary extent. Their subsequent career was, I think, almost entirely her invention. She was aggressive, imaginative, and had a great capacity for ideas, while he was almost destitute of initiative, and could do nothing with ideas except remember and discuss them. She was, if not inexact, at least indolent, with a strong disposition to save energy by sketching—even her handwriting showed that—while she was inexhaustibly industrious with a relentless invariable caligraphy that grew larger and clearer as the years passed by. She had a considerable power of charming; she could be just as nice to people—and incidentally just as nasty—as she wanted to be. He was always just the same, a little confidential and *sotto voce*, artlessly rude and egoistic in an undignified way. She had considerable social experience, good social connections, and considerable social ambition, while he had none of these things. She saw in a flash her opportunity to redeem his defects, use his powers, and do large, novel, rather startling things. She ran him. Her marriage, which shocked her friends and relations beyond measure—for a time they would only speak of Bailey as 'that gnome'—was a stroke of genius, and forthwith they proceeded to make themselves the most formidable and distinguished couple conceivable. P. B. P., she boasted, was engraved inside their wedding rings, Pro Bono Publico, and she meant it to be no idle threat. She had discovered very early that the last thing influential people will do is to work. Everything in their lives tends to make them dependent upon a supply of confidently administered detail. Their business is with the window and not the stock behind, and in the end they are dependent upon the stock behind for what goes into the window. She linked with that the fact Bailey had a mind as orderly as a museum, and an invincible power over detail. She saw that if two people took the necessary pains to know the facts of government and administration with precision, to gather together knowledge that was dispersed and confused, to be able to say precisely what had to be done and what avoided in this eventuality or that, they would necessarily become a centre of reference for all sorts of legislative proposals and political expedients, and she went unhesitatingly upon that.

Bailey, under her vigorous direction, threw up his post in the Civil Service and abandoned sporadic controversies, and they devoted themselves to the elaboration and realisation of this centre of public information she had conceived as their rôle. They set out to study the methods and organisation and realities of government in the most elaborate manner. They did the work as no one had ever hitherto dreamt of doing it. They planned the research on a thoroughly satisfying scale, and arranged their lives almost entirely for it. They took that house in Chambers Street and furnished it with severe economy, they discovered that Scotch domestic who is destined to be the guardian and tyrant of their declining years, and they set to work. Their first book, *The Permanent Official*, fills three plump volumes, and took them and their two secretaries upwards of four years to do. It is an amazingly good book, an enduring achievement. In a hundred directions the history and the administrative treatment of the public service was clarified for all time. . . .

They worked regularly every morning from nine to twelve, they lunched lightly but severely, in the afternoon they 'took exercise' or Bailey attended meetings of the London School Board, on which he served, he said, for the purposes of study—he also became a railway director for the same end. In the late afternoon Altiora was at home to various callers, and in the evening came dinner or a reception or both.

Her dinners and gatherings were a very important feature in their scheme. She got together all sorts of interesting people in or about the public service, she mixed the obscurely efficient with the ill-instructed famous and the rudderless rich, got together in one room more of the factors in our strange jumble of a public life than had ever met easily before. She fed them with a shameless austerity that kept the conversation brilliant, on a soup, a plain fish, and mutton or broiled fowl and milk pudding, with nothing to drink but whisky and soda, and hot and cold water, and milk and lemonade. Everybody was soon very glad indeed to come to that. She boasted how little her housekeeping cost her, and sought constantly for fresh economies that would enable her, she said, to sustain an additional private secretary. Secretaries were the Baileys' one extravagance; they loved to think of searches going on in the British Museum, and letters being cleared up and précis made overhead, while they sat in the little study and worked together, Bailey with a clockwork industry, and Altiora in splendid flashes between intervals of cigarettes and meditation. 'All efficient public careers,' said Altiora, 'consist in the proper direction of secretaries.'

'If everything goes well I shall have another secretary next year,' Altiora told me. 'I wish I could refuse people dinner napkins. Imagine what it means in washing! I dare most things.... But as it is, they stand a lot of hardship here.'

'There's something of the miser in both these people,' said Esmeer, and the thing was perfectly true. For, after all, the miser is nothing more than a man who either through want of imagination or want of suggestion misapplies to a base use a natural power of concentration upon one end. The concentration itself is neither good nor evil, but a power that can be used in either way. And the Baileys gathered and reinvested usuriously not money, but knowledge of the utmost value in human affairs. They produced an effect of having found themselves—completely. One envied them at times extraordinarily. I was attracted, I was dazzled—and at the same time there was something about Bailey's big wrinkled forehead, his lisping broad mouth, the gestures of his hands and an uncivil preoccupation I could not endure....

42 Women and Fiction

From *Granite and Rainbow*

by Virginia Woolf

For notes on Virginia Woolf see under Extract No. 2 The Waves. *This essay was first published in* The Forum *of March 1929. The subject preoccupied Virginia Woolf throughout her literary career.*

Thus it is clear that the extraordinary outburst of fiction in the beginning of the nineteenth century in England was heralded by innumerable slight changes in law and customs and manners. And women of the nineteenth century had some leisure; they had some education. It was no longer the exception for women of the middle and upper classes to choose their own husbands. And it is significant that of the four great women novelists—Jane Austen, Emily Brontë, Charlotte Brontë, and George Eliot—not one had a child, and two were unmarried.

Yet, though it is clear that the ban upon writing had been removed, there was still, it would seem, considerable pressure upon women to write novels. No four women can have been more unlike in genius and character than these four. Jane Austen can have had nothing in common with George Eliot; George Eliot was the direct opposite of Emily Brontë. Yet all were trained for the same profession; all, when they wrote, wrote novels.

Fiction was, as fiction still is, the easiest thing for a woman to write. Nor is it difficult to find the reason. A novel is the least concentrated form of art. A novel can be taken up or put down more easily than a play or a poem. George Eliot left her work to nurse her father. Charlotte Brontë put down her pen to pick the eyes out of the potatoes. And living as she did in the common sitting-room, surrounded by people, a woman was trained to use her mind in observation and upon the analysis of character. She was trained to be a novelist and not to be a poet.

Even in the nineteenth century, a woman lived almost solely in her home and her emotions. And those nineteenth-century novels, remarkable as they were, were profoundly influenced by the fact that the women who wrote them were excluded by their sex from certain kinds of experience. That experience has a great influence upon fiction is indisputable. The best part of Conrad's novels, for instance, would be destroyed if it had been impossible for him to be a sailor. Take away all that Tolstoi knew of war as a soldier, of life and society as a rich young man whose education admitted him to all sorts of experience, and *War and Peace* would be incredibly impoverished.

Yet *Pride and Prejudice*, *Wuthering Heights*, *Villette*, and *Middlemarch* were written by women from whom was forcibly withheld all experience save that which could be met with in a middle-class drawing-room. No first-hand experience of war or seafaring or politics or business was possible for them. Even their emotional life was strictly regulated by law and custom. When George Eliot ventured to live with Mr. Lewes without being his wife, public opinion was scandalised. Under its pressure she withdrew into a suburban seclusion which, inevitably, had the worst possible effects upon her work. She wrote that unless people asked of their own accord to come and see her, she never invited them. At the same time, on the other side of Europe, Tolstoi was living a free life as a soldier, with men and women of all classes, for which nobody censured him and from which his novels drew much of their astonishing breadth and vigour.

But the novels of women were not affected only by the necessarily narrow range of the writer's experience. They showed, at least in the nineteenth century, another characteristic which may be traced to the writer's sex. In *Middlemarch* and in *Jane Eyre* we are conscious not merely of the writer's character, as we are conscious of the character of Charles Dickens, but we are conscious of a woman's presence—of someone resenting the treatment of her sex and pleading for its rights. This brings into women's writing an element which is entirely absent from a man's, unless, indeed, he happens to be a working-man, a negro, or one who for some other reason is conscious of disability. It introduces a distortion and is frequently the cause of weakness. The desire to plead some personal cause or to make a character the mouthpiece of some personal discontent or grievance always has a distressing effect, as if the spot at which the reader's attention is directed were suddenly twofold instead of single.

The genius of Jane Austen and Emily Brontë is never more convincing than in their power to ignore such claims and solicitations and to hold on their way unperturbed by scorn or censure. But it needed a very serene or a very powerful mind to resist the temptation to anger. The ridicule, the censure, the assurance of inferiority in one form or another which were lavished upon women who practised an art, provoked such reactions naturally enough. One sees the effect in Charlotte Brontë's indignation, in George Eliot's resignation. Again and again one finds it in the work of the lesser women writers—in their choice of a subject, in their unnatural self-assertiveness, in their unnatural docility. Moreover, insincerity leaks in almost unconsciously. They adopt a view in deference to authority. The vision becomes too masculine or it becomes too feminine; it loses its perfect integrity and, with that, its most essential quality as a work of art.

It is probable, however, that both in life and in art the values of a woman are not the values of a man. Thus, when a woman comes to write a novel, she will find that she is perpetually wishing to alter the established values—to make serious what appears insignificant to a man, and trivial what is to him important. And for that, of course, she will be criticised; for the critic of the opposite sex will be genuinely puzzled and surprised by an attempt to alter the current scale of values, and will see in it not merely a difference of view, but a view that is weak, or trivial, or sentimental, because it differs from his own.

But here, too, women are coming to be more independent

of opinion. They are beginning to respect their own sense of values. And for this reason the subject matter of their novels begins to show certain changes. They are less interested, it would seem, in themselves; on the other hand, they are more interested in other women. In the early nineteenth century, women's novels were largely autobiographical. One of the motives that led them to write was the desire to expose their own suffering, to plead their own cause. Now that this desire is no longer so urgent, women are beginning to explore their own sex, to write of women as women have never been written of before; for of course, until very lately, women in literature were the creation of men.

Here again there are difficulties to overcome, for, if one may generalise, not only do women submit less readily to observation than men, but their lives are far less tested and examined by the ordinary processes of life. Often nothing tangible remains of a woman's day. The food that has been cooked is eaten; the children that have been nursed have gone out into the world. Where does the accent fall? What is the salient point for the novelist to seize upon? It is difficult to say. Her life has an anonymous character which is baffling and puzzling in the extreme. For the first time, this dark country is beginning to be explored in fiction; and at the same moment a woman has also to record the changes in women's minds and habits which the opening of the professions has introduced. She has to observe how their lives are ceasing to run underground; she has to discover what new colours and shadows are showing in them now that they are exposed to the outer world.

If, then, one should try to sum up the character of women's fiction at the present moment, one would say that it is courageous; it is sincere; it keeps closely to what women feel. It is not bitter. It does not insist upon its femininity. But at the same time, a woman's book is not written as a man would write it. These qualities are much commoner than they were, and they give even to second- and third-rate work the value of truth and the interest of sincerity.

43 Woman in Present Society

From *The Guardian*

by Mary Stott

This article appeared on the Woman's Page of The Guardian, *October 4th 1965.*

Women's organisations, like women's pages of enlightened newspapers, are apt to be sniped at by intelligent young women—and men—for existing at all in this second half of the twentieth century, when men's and women's interests are clearly seen to be so close together in almost every aspect of life. Why do women have to separate themselves off? (You could ask women engineers, women lawyers, women in business, who haven't a tenth of the chance men have of getting to the top; or women factory workers whose average wage has remained at about half men's, ever since records were kept.. though that isn't my point just now.) Isn't getting together as *women*, emphasising that women think differently, feel differently, about human problems, whether deprived children or nuclear warfare, just prolonging this tedious old sex war? Isn't it time we all thought and fought together, as human beings?

Perhaps it is. I'd rather like to think I shall live long enough to see separate women's organisations die of inanition. But when that day comes, as I'm sure it will, one good thing will be lost—the possibility of a nationwide pressure group which unites in amicable understanding and cooperation people of strongly opposed religious, social, and political views. A national organisation of men on these lines is an impossibility, an absurdity. But because women found their voice as *women*, pleading, fighting, for higher education, for a vote, for entry to the professions, for social reforms affecting women as housewives, mothers, and workers, a nationwide, nonpolitical, nonsectarian pressure group of women is not an impossibility, and far from being an absurdity. In a way, it exists in the Women's Institutes. It has certainly existed for seventy years in the National Council of Women.

The N.C.W.'s list of affiliated organisations gives a fascinating picture of the social history of Britain. There are the relics of the powerful suffrage and fighting feminist societies—the National Women's Citizens Association, the Open Door Council, the Fawcett Society, named after that great suffragist Dame Millicent Garrett Fawcett. There is the Women's Co-operative Guild, founded in 1883, the first organization to coax working-class women out of the four walls of home. There are half-forgotten crusading bodies like the British Women's Temperance Association. There are the professional women's organisations from the Royal College of Nurses and Royal College of Midwives, to the newish professions of home economists and physiotherapists. There are the recent mixed organisations like the Marriage Guidance Council and the Family Planning Association.

Clearly the National Council of Women is not a relic. It is still steadily recruiting young women, young organisations ... organisations formed only in the last few years, like the National Childbirth Trust, the National Association of Pre-School Playgroups. When Megan du Boisson formed her Disablement Incomes Group, one of the first bodies she approached for support and guidance was the National Council of Women and I believe recommendations on the lines she advocates appear in the memorandum the N.C.W. has sent to the Government's inquiry into the whole field of social security.

The National Council of Women embraces the Mothers' Union, the Union of Catholic Mothers, the League of Jewish Women, the Free Church Women's Council, and the Salvation Army; the women's advisory committees of the Labour Party and the Conservative and Unionist Associations, and the Women's Liberal Association; the Anglican

Group for the Ordination of Women to the Historic Ministry of the Church, the Horses and Ponies Protection Association, and the Guild of Lady Drivers. Can anything useful and practical—above the level of 'identification of streets and houses', which is a resolution down for discussion at the annual conference at Portsmouth next week—possibly come out of such a hotch-potch of interests?

Yes. It can and it does. I have no doubt that the hard, sustained work of the National Council of Women for example, was the major factor in persuading the Government to lift the earnings rule for widows. When 'clarification of the abortion law' is discussed at Portsmouth, I believe something sensible, some small step forward, will be agreed, in spite of the fact that there will be delegates from the Catholic Mothers and from the Abortion Law Reform Association. Universality does *not* mean impotence. As Roosevelt said. 'Politics is the art of the impossible.' Bring together a number of sensible people, experienced as magistrates, councillors, social workers, leaders of their professions, careful of facts, all concerned with the common good, and they will find some basis of agreement, even if it is less than the crusaders would want. By such small steps we move forward.

'A Parliament of women' is a phrase that makes some people wince. But a parliament of responsible citizens without Whips is another story. Aren't women rather lucky to have still this common ground of their sex? And to be able to meet together and discuss in a civilised way what has to be done without party sneers, political acrimony? It's a thought, isn't it?

Suggestions for Oral Discussion or Written Work

General Questions

1. How has the education of girls changed since the days of Jane Eyre? (*Jane Eyre* was written in the 1840's but refers to the first years of the nineteenth century.)
2. Compare Jane Eyre and Dorothea of *Middlemarch* in their attitude to life.
3. Do you think the education of girls has changed since the days of Mary Kingsley? (Last half of the nineteenth century.)
4. If girls now have better educational opportunities why should there be so much dissatisfaction? Perhaps you do not agree that there is any dissatisfaction. Read the 'women's pages' of *The Guardian* or *The Times* for a few weeks and see if you can find the causes of the tension suffered by the 'educated' woman.
5. Who, of all the women writing or written of in this book would you most like to have been, and why?
6. Which authors have made you want to read more of their work?
7. Leaving aside the 'documentary' aspects of the extracts, can you compare the styles of any three of the women writers with three of the men writers and say that there is a definite 'feminine' mode of thinking?

Particular Questions

1. *The House in Paris:* From your own experience do you think that what Elizabeth Bowen says is true?
2. *The Waves:* Can you characterise the three girls?
3. *Memoirs of a Dutiful Daughter:* Have you ever regretted being born a woman? If so, why? If not, why not?
4. *The Member of the Wedding:* Have you ever felt like

this? What do you think was the matter with Frankie, if anything?
5 *The Rainbow:* What 'vision' is the author speaking about?
6a *The Story of an African Farm:* Are these sentiments echoed by any other woman in this book?
 b *The Story of an African Farm:* Compare this extract with No. 8 (Marie Bashkirtseff). Have the narrator and the diarist anything in common?
7 *Jane Eyre:* Was Jane Eyre 'typical' or just herself? (If you have read the book.)
8 *Marie Bashkirtseff—Journals:* Marie was unlike most of us in that she had especial talent, particularly for painting. Would a girl's feelings be the same if she knew she was ordinary?
9 *Mary Kingsley—Letters:* Do you think Charlotte Brontë and Mary Kingsley would have had anything to talk about together? (Mrs. Gaskell's *Life of Charlotte Brontë* might interest you. *The Life of Mary Kingsley* by Stephen Gwynn and *Victorian Lady Travellers* edited by Dorothy Middleton will give you information about Miss Kingsley.)
10. *A Vindication of the Rights of Women:* Have women's rights been vindicated?
11 *Emma:* From this extract could you give a friend a description of Emma's personality?
12 *Middlemarch:* Would your ideal husband be anything like Dorothea's?
13 *Agnes Grey:* Why was a governess's life so difficult? What qualities were necessary to be a successful one? Were Agnes Grey's problems any different from those of some teachers today?
However far do you think Agnes Grey's failure as a governess was due to nineteenth century educational methods or to 'original sin'?
14 *The Egoist:* Analyse Meredith's style. Do you like it?
15 *Portrait of a Lady:* Sum up Isabel's feelings for her husband. Can you describe him from what Isabel herself thinks?

16 *Letters: Jane Austen* Has Jane Austen herself 'common sense'?
   Which author in the book might *not* agree with her about emotional problems?
17 *Queen Victoria: Letters:* Do you think these attitudes are still common?
18 *At the Bay:* Do you think Linda's was a satisfactory marriage?
19 *To the Lighthouse:* What has the style of this extract in common with No. 2?
20 *Letters: Jane Welsh Carlyle:* Did you enjoy reading this?
   What characteristics would you say Jane Welsh Carlyle possessed?
21 *All Passion Spent:* Can you write an imaginary portrait of Henry?
22 *A View of the Harbour:* Would this woman have the same worries in the nineteenth century?
23 *The Little Ottleys:* What is different about this writer in comparison with the previous five or six?
24 *Dangerous Ages:* This was written forty years ago. Have things changed since then?
25 *A Doll's House:* Why do you think this play caused such a stir in 1879?
26 *The Holiday:* Did you enjoy reading this?
27 *The Echoing Grove:* Do you think Madeline is unhappy only because she has been jilted?
28 *Howard's End:* Has anything fundamentally changed about this situation?
29 *The Woodlanders:* Do you think it is easier to be good if you are simple and uneducated?
30 *Letters to Imlay:* cf No. 10 also. What sort of person do you think Mary Wollstonecraft was? Find out all you can about her. Look up under Mary Wollstonecraft—*Godwin*.
31 *Middlemarch:* Would you have liked to be married to Lydgate?
32 & 33 *An Ideal Husband:* How does the dramatist get his effects?
   What sort of society do his characters move in?

34 *Man and Superman:* Is Jack Tanner like anyone you have ever met?
35 *My Life:* Could you attempt a portrait of the writer from the style of the extract?
36 *A Proper Marriage:* Did Martha enjoy being a mother? Which qualities do you think are necessary to be a good one?
37 *Liber Amoris:* Could a woman have written this? (Presuming the object of her love was a man.)
38 *Look the other Way:* Is this a realistic description of modern family life?
39 *Nightmare Abbey:* Do you find this funny?
40 *A Room of One's Own:* Do you think this is what would have happened?
41 *The New Machiavelli:* Altiora is a thinly-veiled satirical portrait of Mrs. Beatrice Webb. What do you think 'muliebrity' is and why should such a feminist as Wells obviously like it?
Do you think Altiora and her husband were well suited?
42 *Granite and Rainbow:* Discuss with reference to novels by women which you have read.
43 *The Guardian:* Summarise the argument and discuss some of the organisations mentioned.

Suggestions for Further Reading

Margot Asquith: *Off the Record; Autobiography.*
Diana Athill: *Instead of a Letter.*
Jane Austen: *Love and Friendship; Pride and Prejudice; Sense and Sensibility; Northanger Abbey; Persuasion.*
Arnold Bennett: *The Old Wives' Tale.*
Lesley Blanch: *The Wilder Shores of Love; The Sabres of Paradise.*
Elizabeth Bowen: *The Death of the Heart; A World of Love; The Heat of the Day; The Little Girls.*
Vera Brittain: *Testament of Youth.*
Charlotte Brontë: *The Professor; Shirley; Villette.*
Emily Brontë: *Wuthering Heights.*
Fanny Burney: *Evelina; Diary.*
Daniel Defoe: *Moll Flanders.*
Margaret Drabble: *The Millstone.*
George Eliot: *The Mill on the Floss* et al.
E. M. Forster: *Passage to India; Where Angels Fear to Tread.*
E. C. Gaskell: *Cranford; Wives and Daughters; Mary Barton; North and South.*
Jane Gillespie: *The Weir; Envy; A Pot of Basil; Made for Love; Family Feeling* and many others.
Elinor Glyn: *Autobiography.*
L. P. Hartley: *The Shrimp and the Anemone; The Sixth Heaven; Eustace and Hilda.*
Joan Haslip: *Lady Hester Stanhope* (Biography).
Nathaniel Hawthorne: *The Scarlet Letter.*
Aldous Huxley: *Antic Hay; Point Counterpoint.*
Henry James: *Portrait of a Lady.*
D. H. Lawrence: *Sons and Lovers; Women in Love; The Lost Girl.*
R. Lehmann: *Dusty Answer; The Ballad and the Source; Invitation to the Waltz.*
Doris Lessing: *Martha Quest; A Ripple in the Storm; The Golden Notebook*—and any of her collections of short stories.
Ada Leverson: Ed. C. Macinnes—*The Little Ottleys* (collected volume of novels).

Mary Macarthy: *Memoirs of a Catholic Girlhood; The Group.*
Katherine Mansfield: *Journal; Letters; Bliss,* (short stories).
George Meredith: *The Tragic Comedians.*
Ed. D. Middleton: *Victorian Lady Travellers.*
George Moore: *Esther Waters.*
Charles Morgan: *The Fountain.*
Doris Langley Moore: *E. Nesbit* (Biography).
Florence Nightingale: *Letters* (collected edition 2 vols.).
George Orwell: *The Clergyman's Daughter.*
Hester Piozzi (Mrs. Thrale) and Penelope Pennington: *Letters.*
Dorothy Richardson: *Pilgrimage.* (New edition in four volumes.)
Henry Handel Richardson: *Myself When Young; The Getting of Wisdom.*
J. D. Salinger: *Franny and Zooey; To Esmé with Love and Squalor.*
G. B. Shaw: *Letters* (new edition, vol. 1); *The Apple Cart; St. Joan.*
Edith Sitwell: *Taken Care Of (Autobiography)*
Stevie Smith: *Novel on Yellow Paper.*
A. Strindberg: *Miss Julie.*
Elizabeth Taylor: *A Wreath of Roses; Palladian; A Game of Hide and Seek; The Sleeping Beauty; The Soul of Kindness;*
Life of St. Teresa (Penguin edition).
W. M. Thackeray: *Vanity Fair; Henry Esmond.*
John Updike: *Rabbit Run.*
Hugh Walpole: *The Golden Scarecrow; The Herries Chronicles.*
Evelyn Waugh: *Vile Bodies; Decline and Fall.*
Beatrice Webb: *My Apprenticeship; Our Partnership.*
H. G. Wells: *Ann Veronica; Autobiography.*
Angus Wilson: *The Middle Age of Mrs. Eliot.*
Virginia Woolf: *Mrs. Dalloway; The Common Reader (*2 vols.), etc.
Dorothy Wordsworth: *Home at Grasmere* (Penguin edition of extracts from her journals).

For Product Safety Concerns and Information please contact our EU representative GPSR@taylorandfrancis.com
Taylor & Francis Verlag GmbH, Kaufingerstraße 24, 80331 München, Germany

www.ingramcontent.com/pod-product-compliance
Lightning Source LLC
Chambersburg PA
CBHW070724020526
44116CB00031B/1795